What People Are Saying About
James Goll and *Impacting the World Through Spiritual Gifts*…

Ever since my friend James Goll was set on fire by the Holy Spirit, he has been a demonstrator of the grace and power of God's Spirit. Now, for the first time, he teaches the field-tested secrets he has learned so that you can release the gifts of the Spirit in your life. Now is the time for you, too, to experience the fire of the Holy Spirit and to operate in the gifts. If not now, when?

—*Sid Roth*
Host, *It's Supernatural!*

James Goll's study guide *Impacting the World Through Spiritual Gifts* is an excellent, well-written work. I like how he drew from different streams instead of just representing one stream or denominational viewpoint. James is a diligent student of the Word of God and the ways of God. His years of experience and years of study are reflected in this book. I love to be around bright people who are full of the Spirit and who value hearing from God. James was the first prophet whom I sat with and asked for prayer and activation in the prophetic. I sense God is readying the church for a new visitation. When He comes near, we experience more of His grace as empowerment through the expressions of grace seen in the gifts of the Holy Spirit. I sense this is the hour to no longer be satisfied with knowing about the grace gifts of God—God wants us to understand how to hear from Him and to act on His behalf through His divine enablements, His gifts. I am grateful to James for this labor of love that helps to clarify for many who are just now coming to the Master's banquet table the importance and the value of His gifts, and the way to begin flowing and growing in them.

—*Randy Clark, D. Min.*
Founder and president of Global Awakening and the Apostolic Network of Global Awakening

James Goll has provided us with an excellent study guide that will give both student and scholar much to consider. How many times have we wished we had a clear, concise study guide for today's church to instruct us in the gifts of the Holy Spirit! Now we have one! *Impacting the World Through Spiritual Gifts* will activate your gifts and give you a desire to release them to the body of Christ with wisdom and grace. More than just a study guide, this is a book full of insight from a true friend of the Holy Spirit. You'll want more than one copy to share with your friends, your home study group, your church!

—*Dr. Brian Simmons*
The Passion Translation Project
Stairway Ministries

Dr. James Goll is one of the most thorough teachers in our day on subjects pertaining to the Spirit of God and kingdom life. His teachings are prophetically inspired, and yet any academically motivated individual will truly sit down to a feast when they use his materials and receive a prophetic infusion at the same time. The gifts of the Spirit is a subject dear to my heart as it was the first official training I received as a new believer. In this study guide, James does a brilliant job of empowering the hungry student in both understanding and activating these wonderful kingdom tools.

—*Patricia King*
Founder, XP Ministries
www.patriciaking.com

Dr. James Goll is a forerunner and pioneer in the prophetic and apostolic movements, impacting the nations for decades with his dynamic teachings and deep spiritual insights. *Impacting the World Through Spiritual Gifts* builds on the rich legacy of the Holy Spirit evident in the life and ministry of Dr. Goll. This is more than a book; it is a supernatural activation tool for every believer. Through the pages of this supernatural manual, believers will receive revelatory teaching on how to recognize, activate, and release the gifts of the Holy Spirit in their lives. Contrary to popular belief, the gifts of the Spirit are not static but require our active participation and partnership. This divinely inspired book will answer your vital questions, such as: "Are the gifts of the Spirit relevant for today?" "How do I become more sensitive to the Holy Spirit?" "How do believers release the power of the Holy Spirit in their lives?" If you are ready to walk in a greater dimension of the supernatural, this book is for you! Read with intentionality and hunger, and you will never be the same again!

—*Kynan T. Bridges*
Founder and president of Kynan Bridges Ministries, Inc.
Pastor, Grace & Peace Global Fellowship
International best-selling author

James Goll has been operating in the gifts of the Spirit for decades. Now, he's blending sound theology with practical experience to help you press into the supernatural in this valuable study guide. Whether you are a soccer mom who, as Paul admonishes us in 1 Corinthians 12:31, earnestly desires spiritual gifts or a minister who wants to root the operations of these gifts firmly in Scripture, *Impacting the World Through Spiritual Gifts* equips, inspires, and activates you to understand and press into the Holy Spirit's gifts. Every Christian needs to read this book!

—*Jennifer LeClaire*
Senior editor, *Charisma* magazine
Director, Awakening House of Prayer

James Goll's new study guide is a must for those who want to grow in the areas of hearing the voice of God and developing the gifts of the Spirit in their lives. I have had the honor of ministering with this dear man and observing him teach, impart, and activate others into their destiny. By reading this book, you will be activated in a supernatural anointing made natural in your life today!

—*Jerame Nelson*
Living At His Feet Ministries
Author, *Encountering Angels* and *Burning Ones*

I've always considered James Goll to be one of the main fathers of the modern-day prophetic movement. And just when I think he's exhausted what he might teach on the spiritual gifts today, he creates even better resources—including this study guide and its related book, *Releasing Spiritual Gifts Today*—with the quality of university-level documentation. These works *have* to be the most comprehensive, best-documented materials on learning to both receive and operate in the biblical spiritual gifts available today. I daresay there is not a Scripture reference missing on the subject. Whether you are new to the subject or highly seasoned, you are about to discover a wealth of more biblical research than has ever before been at your fingertips!

—*Steve Shultz*
Founder, The Elijah List
Author, *Can You Speak Louder?*

James Goll is one of the most brilliant yet simple and down-to-earth leaders I know. We've been taught, taught, taught! Now James is rallying the call to release, release, release…spiritual gifts. *Impacting the World Through Spiritual Gifts* is so clear that releasing becomes simple. Just do it. And find someone to do it with. Releasing becomes contagious. This book will transform you into a DOER!

—*Barbara J. Yoder*
Lead Apostle, Shekinah Regional Apostolic Center, Ann Arbor, MI
Author, *The Breaker Anointing* and many other books

Natural ability and talents are great and are God-given. But your natural talents aren't enough to fulfill the divine purpose and calling God has for you. You need the anointing and operation of the Holy Spirit to be able to do all God has called you to do. *Impacting the World Through Spiritual Gifts* will empower you to operate in a new level of spiritual gifting and power! In this study guide, James Goll masterfully teaches on the subject of functioning in all nine gifts of the Holy Spirit, including the gifts of revelation, power, and utterance. He teaches in a clear, organized, and powerful way. Not only will you learn what the gifts of the Spirit are, but you will also learn practical steps to seeing these manifestations of God increase in and through you. You will be equipped to impact the lives of those around you with the power of the Holy Spirit. I highly recommend this book for individuals, home groups, churches, Bible studies, and Bible schools. It will be a great resource in your spiritual arsenal!

—*Matt Sorger*
Prophetic healing revivalist
TV host and author, *Power for Life*
mattsorger.com

James Goll walks his talk and demonstrates what he teaches. I know this man and his teachings. We have served on each other's ministry boards for several years. James has given the body of Christ a great tool by presenting these spiritual truths in a manner that is understandable and yet filled with a depth of Scripture/historical precedent mixed with modern-day examples. If you believe that Jesus Christ is the same, yesterday, today and forever, then you are going to love *Impacting the World Through Spiritual Gifts*!

—*Elizabeth Alves*
Founder, Increase International
International best-selling author, *Mighty Prayer Warrior*

FOREWORD BY CHÉ AHN

JAMES W. GOLL

IMPACTING
THE WORLD THROUGH
SPIRITUAL
Gifts

WHITAKER
HOUSE

IMPACTING THE WORLD THROUGH SPIRITUAL GIFTS

James W. Goll
Encounters Network
P.O. Box 1653
Franklin, TN 37065
www.encountersnetwork.com • www.prayerstorm.com
www.compassionacts.com • www.GETeSchool.com
info@encountersnetwork.com • inviteJames@gmail.com

ISBN: 978-1-62911-706-5
eBook ISBN: 978-1-62911-607-5
Printed in the United States of America
© 2016 by James W. Goll

Whitaker House
1030 Hunt Valley Circle
New Kensington, PA 15068
www.whitakerhouse.com

1 2 3 4 5 6 7 8 9 10 11 ᙄ 23 22 21 20 19 18 17 16

ACKNOWLEDGMENTS AND DEDICATION

Impacting the World Through Spiritual Gifts has been developed from the gleanings of the ministries of others. Over the years, I have endeavored to be a student of many of the different streams of the movements of the Holy Spirit that have flowed through the church of Jesus Christ. These pages reflect that study.

In particular, I want to acknowledge the friendship and ministry of Mahesh and Bonnie Chavda, who have given me so much. I learned a great deal about the gift of discerning of spirits through Pat Gastineau of Word of Love in Roswell, Georgia, and I was exposed to the gift of faith through the late Kenneth Hagin, as well as other spiritual pioneers. I thank the Lord for the teaching ministry of Jim Croft, the groundbreaking exploration of signs and wonders of John Wimber, and the apostolic teaching first of Derek Prince and then of C. Peter Wagner.

In the pages that follow, I acknowledge the contributions of several of these friends who have written books on the topic of spiritual gifts, along with Sam Storms, Dick Iverson, and Mel Robeck. I have also benefited greatly from the prophetic impartations of John Sanford, Cindy Jacobs, Bill Hamon, the late Bob Jones, and several others.

First and foremost, I am thankful to our Father for sending us the precious Holy Spirit, the third person of the Godhead, who is our greatest gift! Therefore, with a grateful heart, I dedicate this book to the work and ministry of the Holy Spirit. You are our Comforter, our Guide, our Fruit-bearer, and our Gift-bringer. Come, Holy Spirit, and empower Your people anew!

CONTENTS

Foreword by Ché Ahn...11

Preface: Just Do It! 13

SECTION ONE: INTRODUCTION TO SPIRITUAL GIFTS...........................15

    Lesson One: What Are the Spiritual Gifts? 16

    Lesson Two: How the Holy Spirit Moves 27

    Lesson Three: How to Grow in Exercising Spiritual Gifts 36

SECTION TWO: REVELATORY GIFTS—THE GIFTS THAT REVEAL..............45

    Lesson Four: The Gift of Discerning of Spirits....................46

    Lesson Five: The Gift of a Word of Wisdom 56

    Lesson Six: The Gift of a Word of Knowledge 65

SECTION THREE: POWER GIFTS—THE GIFTS THAT DO......................75

    Lesson Seven: The Gift of Faith....................................76

    Lesson Eight: The Gifts of Healings................................85

    Lesson Nine: The Workings of Miracles 94

SECTION FOUR: VOCAL GIFTS—THE GIFTS THAT SPEAK 105

    Lesson Ten: The Gift of Various Kinds of Tongues 106

    Lesson Eleven: The Gift of Interpretation of Tongues 115

    Lesson Twelve: The Gift of Prophecy...............................124

Closing Exhortation: Fulfilling the Great Commission Today 135

Notes 137

Answers to Questions for Reflection 139

Recommended Resources...142

FOREWORD

When Jesus' followers gathered in Jerusalem to receive *"the Promise of the Father"* (Acts 1:4 NKJV), they waited with open hearts to welcome this movement of God in their lives, not fully understanding what was coming. What they received—what was poured out into their lives from heaven—was a Person, God the Holy Spirit. And with the Promise of the Father came clear manifestations of His presence within them and among them: a powerful wind, tongues of fire, and an ability to speak in languages unknown to them but known to those who were listening to them, as they joyfully proclaimed God's wonderful works of salvation and life. The results were beyond what the disciples could ever have imagined, as three thousand people gave their lives to Christ in one day and the message of the gospel was carried to regions and countries well beyond Jerusalem.

Jesus gives a variety of gifts to His church to provide ongoing comfort, exhortation, and encouragement for His people. *"When He ascended on high, He led captivity captive, and gave gifts to men"* (Ephesians 4:8 NKJV). The gifts of the Spirit build up and strengthen God's people. They establish us in His love, enable us to serve one another's needs, and empower us to be living demonstrations of the gospel of Jesus Christ to the world around us. But the essence of the gifts is the Person who gives them, the One who pours out God's unconditional love and life-giving grace.

Whenever we open our hearts to welcome the Spirit anew into our individual and corporate lives—whenever we appreciate and honor Him, hosting His presence—He will manifest God's glory in our midst, bringing hope, peace, power, and a renewed vision to build God's kingdom on earth. The fullness of life in the body of Christ is offered to us through the Giver and His gifts. We will miss out on so much of His comfort, strength, and encouragement until we learn to release His gifts in our lives—*today*. And when we release God's power and presence into the world, people will be transformed in ways we never imagined possible.

In *Impacting the World Through Spiritual Gifts*, James Goll invites you to know and appreciate the gifts of the Spirit and to clearly understand what it means for you to release them. With solid biblical teaching, insights from noted Christian leaders, stirring testimonies, and personal application, he opens for you the realm of the supernatural, where the movement of the Spirit is the norm, where people see the glory of God, and where healing and wholeness are restored to individuals and communities.

This supernatural life is available to you today as God's gifts are released through you. Use this guide with an open heart and a discerning mind. You will receive a fresh infilling of the Promise of the Father, enabling you to pour out the life of God for salvation, healing, miraculous works, supernatural guidance, and pure worship.

—*Dr. Ché Ahn*
Apostle, Harvest Apostolic Center, Pasadena, California
Senior pastor, HRock Church
President, Harvest International Ministry
International Chancellor, Wagner Leadership Institute

PREFACE: JUST DO IT!

I have intentionally titled this study guide *Impacting the World Through Spiritual Gifts* rather than "Receiving Spiritual Gifts" because I believe we should *do* something with spiritual gifts now—not just study them in order to learn what they are and how to obtain them. Giving God's love to others by means of His gifts presupposes first having received them, and it is important to learn how to use the gifts of His Spirit today rather than merely learn how to receive them and then sit on our hands and do nothing with them!

Not long ago, "the gifts of the Holy Spirit" was a hot topic, and most of the books about spiritual gifts that are available were published in the recent past. Yet even though you will not hear as much preaching and teaching about them these days, God has not rescinded His gifts or His commissioning. He has not lifted these special manifestations of His grace. Rather, in these latter days that we are living in, He has determined to pour them forth *all the more*, with even greater degrees of impact and authority. God not only wants you to learn about His gifts, but He also wants you to experience the great wonder of moving in and through His grace on a daily basis. Experience, under the direction of the Holy Spirit, will be your best tutor; and you can expect to keep learning as you keep on doing—today, tomorrow, and the next day. Practice does make perfect! As the popular slogan goes, "Just do it!"

The Nine Most Widely Recognized Gifts

Impacting the World Through Spiritual Gifts is divided into four sections, with three lessons in each part. The first section gives you an overview of spiritual gifts and introduces you to the way the Holy Spirit moves and operates through them. Sections two through four give you specific information about the nine most widely recognized spiritual gifts, grouped together as "Revelatory Gifts," "Power Gifts," and "Vocal Gifts."

Section two, "Revelatory Gifts," describes three gifts that "reveal": discerning of spirits, word of wisdom, and word of knowledge. Section three, "Power Gifts," examines three gifts that "do": faith, healings, and workings of miracles. Last, but not least, "Vocal Gifts" covers three gifts that "speak," or gifts that rely on the human vocal cords for manifestation: tongues, interpretation of tongues, and prophecy.

These nine gifts are not the only gifts God gives to His children, but they are vital ones to learn about, to understand, and to activate as He leads.

Throughout, I give you plenty of examples of these spiritual gifts in action, both in current, everyday life and within the pages of the Bible. It is always exciting to see God working through His people; and even when we revisit familiar biblical stories, we can always see something new in them.

Information, Inspiration, and Impartation

My three main purposes for this study guide are *information*, *inspiration*, and *impartation*. First, that the information presented here will bring you into a greater awareness of biblical truth about spiritual gifts. Second, that you will be inspired, through the personal and biblical stories, to greater levels of hope and faith regarding the tremendous potential of the gifts God has given to you. Third, that you will be imparted by the Spirit with the courage to step forward and use them.

It is my hope that all of us will study to show ourselves approved as effective workers for our Master. I base this goal on 2 Timothy 2:15, which reads, *"Be diligent to present yourself approved to God as a workman who does not need to be ashamed, accurately handling the word of truth."* The Lord has gifted each and every one of us. May He be magnified in our lives as we serve as His hands and feet and voice in the world around us.

Nothing will happen if you don't step out in faith. Let the lessons you are about to study stir you to respond anew to His direction so that you can "just do it"—use the spiritual gifts that God gives you—every day of your life. Remember, faith is spelled R-I-S-K, and the best fruit is always way out there on the end of the limb! What does the Lord want to do for you and through you? Let's turn the page and see what He has in store for you today.

INTRODUCTION TO SPIRITUAL GIFTS

"Jesus Christ is the same yesterday and today and forever."
—Hebrews 13:8

The Holy Spirit is at work everywhere in the world, and all of His gifts are still fully operational in the lives of believers. These gifts are not ours to simply play with or ignore according to our whims. They are ours to activate by faith and to use at His direction.

God gives spiritual gifts so that everyone can profit from them, so that each member of the body of Christ can benefit the others. The gifts operate similarly to the functioning of the human body, where each part and organ works together with the others so the whole body can flourish. It is impossible to have a glorious, fully functioning body of Christ apart from the *charismata*, the gifts of the Spirit.

WHAT ARE THE SPIRITUAL GIFTS?

"To each one is given the manifestation of the Spirit for the common good."
—1 Corinthians 12:7

I. INTRODUCTORY STATEMENTS

A. John Wimber (late author, international Vineyard leader)

Spiritual gifts are the expression of God's power at work in the Church today. A believer does not possess gifts; a believer receives gifts from God to be used at special times for special occasions. Gifts are the attestation of the empowering of the Holy Spirit and are vital in a "signs and wonders" ministry.

Spiritual empowering equips one for service. The gifts are the tools which enable one to fulfill the ministry required.

The gifts of the Spirit are received by impartation. The gifts (except the private use of tongues) are given to us and through us to use for others, and are developed in a climate of risk-taking and willingness to fail.[1]

B. Mel Robeck (Fuller Theological Seminary professor)

The gifts (*charismata*) of the Holy Spirit are the transrational [going beyond human reason] manifestations of God. They are given by God for the purpose of ministry taking place for the good of the Body of Christ (1 Corinthians 12:7).

The *source* of the gifts is the Holy Spirit (1 Corinthians 12; Hebrews 2:4).

The *recipients* are the community of the Spirit, sometimes called the people of God or the Body of Christ (1 Corinthians 12; Romans 12; Ephesians 4; 1 Peter 4:10–11).

16

Their *purpose* is to edify the Body, equip the saints, and glorify God.

Their *motive* should always be love (1 Corinthians 13:1–13).

The way and wherefore of spiritual gifts is directly related to the work of the Holy Spirit throughout history.[2]

C. Dick Iverson (author, founding pastor of City Bible Church [Oregon], formerly called Portland Bible Temple)

[The gifts of the Holy Spirit] are not just human talents, or even human abilities energized by the Holy Spirit. The gifts are direct manifestations of the Holy Spirit through believers. God does use human abilities and He does energize them with His Spirit, but that is something different than the gifts of the Spirit. It may also be true that God equips us by personality and temperament to match the gifts in which we function, yet the actual function of the gifts is beyond the personality and ability of the [person], they function by the supernatural influence and operation of the Holy Spirit.[3]

D. Derek Prince (late author, international Bible teacher)

The gifts of the Holy Spirit are the supernaturally imparted abilities to do the works of Jesus. Each of the twenty-five New Testament charismata is an example of grace made specific, effective, and manifest. These gifts are a manifestation of the Holy Spirit within a believer. No believer should be without his own distinctive manifestations of the Holy Spirit. We are exhorted to seek all the spiritual gifts.

E. Peter Wagner (missiologist, author, apostolic teacher)

A spiritual gift is a special attribute given by the Holy Spirit to every member of the Body of Christ, according to God's grace, for use within the context of the Body.[4]

(Note that Peter does not mean gifts are inward-looking alone—meant only for use within the church and for the mutual benefit of Christians. Whenever and wherever the church ministers, both inwardly and outwardly, ministry is best conducted through gifted believers.)

II. PURPOSES OF THE GIFTS OF THE SPIRIT

A. For the Common Good

To each one is given the manifestation of the Spirit for the common good.

(1 Corinthians 12:7)

The apostle Paul made it clear that we are to use our spiritual gifts to benefit the local body of which we are a member:

> *But to each one is given the manifestation of the Spirit for the common good. For to one is given the word of wisdom through the Spirit, and to another the word of knowledge according to the same Spirit; to another faith by the same Spirit, and to another gifts of healing by the one Spirit, and to another the effecting of miracles, and to another prophecy, and to another the distinguishing ["discerning" NKJV] of spirits, to another various kinds of tongues, and to another the interpretation of tongues. But one and the same Spirit works all these things, distributing to each one individually just as He wills.*
>
> (1 Corinthians 12:7–11)

> *Even so you, since you are zealous for spiritual gifts, let it be for the edification of the church that you seek to excel.*   (1 Corinthians 14:12 NKJV)

B.   To Form a Body

The body of Christ is not just a gathering of believers; it is the living body of the Lord Jesus Christ on earth today. God gives spiritual gifts so that the entire body of Christ can profit from them, so that each member can benefit the others. It's like the human body, where each part and organ works together with the others so that the whole body can flourish.

> *Now you are Christ's body, and individually members of it.*   (1 Corinthians 12:27)

Each of us has been gifted for the sake of others. The nine gifts of the Spirit described in detail in this study guide are not the totality of body ministry, but total body ministry is not possible without them.

C.   To Accompany the Preaching of the Gospel

It is impossible to have a glorious, fully functioning body of Christ apart from the *charismata*, the gifts of the Spirit. Without supernatural endowments, the church cannot presume to preach the gospel to the whole world and to reap the great harvest prior to the coming of the Lord. Another way of saying it is that the gospel is not being fully preached unless it is *"with signs following"* (Mark 16:20 KJV).

1.   *Therefore in Christ Jesus I have found reason for boasting in things pertaining to God. For I will not presume to speak of anything except what Christ has accomplished through me, resulting in the obedience of the Gentiles by word and deed, in the power of signs and wonders, in the power of the Spirit; so that from Jerusalem and round about as far as Illyricum I have fully preached the gospel of Christ.*   (Romans 15:17–20)

2.   *My message and my preaching were not in persuasive words of wisdom, but in demonstration of the Spirit and of power.*   (1 Corinthians 2:4)

3.   *And the crowds with one accord paid attention to what was being said by Philip when they heard him and saw the signs that he did.*   (Acts 8:6 ESV)

4. *How will we escape if we neglect so great a salvation? After it was at the first spoken through the Lord, it was confirmed to us by those who heard, God also testifying with them, both by signs and wonders and by various miracles and by gifts of the Holy Spirit according to His own will.* (Hebrews 2:3–4)

D. Testimony—Sabrina

While teaching in the nation of Albania, right after Communism was lifted, I had a powerful experience where the gifts of the Holy Spirit were in operation, resulting in the salvation and healing of many.

Through my interpreter, I began to preach about how God sets us free from rejection and oppression, and I told a little bit about my background and testimony. After I launched into my sermon, I kept speaking for a while, although I could see I wasn't getting much of anywhere. Then the name *Sarah* floated through my mind. That was the second time it had happened that day, and I had to assume that God had given it to me for a reason. I turned to my interpreter and asked, "How do you say the name Sarah in the Albanian language?"

My interpreter said, "Sabrina." So, I asked if there was a lady there named Sabrina. Sure enough, there was. The Holy Spirit proceeded to give me her age and a word of knowledge that she had a tumor in her left breast. With a gift of faith, I stated that Jesus wanted to heal her.

No one in the gathering had ever heard the gospel of Jesus before. But everyone present knew Sabrina, and they watched as she gave her heart to Jesus. Everything I had said was accurate. This resulted in a dramatic move of the Holy Spirit in which people were saved, healed, and delivered of evil spirits. Jesus was magnified that night, and a true move of the Holy Spirit was triggered by one word of knowledge.

III. GIFTS THROUGH IMPARTATION

God's gifts are received by impartation in at least three ways (and perhaps more):

A. Sovereignly Given

God gives grace, gifts, ministries, and offices as He desires. His decision to bestow gifts is not dependent on human preparation or choosing but rather on God's sovereign election and choice.

1. *When the Day of Pentecost had fully come, they were all with one accord in one place. And suddenly there came a sound from heaven, as of a rushing mighty wind, and it filled the whole house where they were sitting. Then there appeared to them divided tongues, as of fire, and one sat upon each of them. And they were all filled with the Holy Spirit and began to speak with other tongues, as the Spirit gave them utterance.* (Acts 2:1–4 NKJV)

2. *Now the full number of those who believed were of one heart and soul, and no one said that any of the things that belonged to him was his own, but they had everything in*

common. And with great power the apostles were giving their testimony to the resurrec-
tion of the Lord Jesus, and great grace was upon them all.   (Acts 4:32–33 ESV)

3. *While Peter was still speaking these words, the Holy Spirit fell upon all those who were*
    listening to the message.   (Acts 10:44)

B. Laying On of Hands

Those who are already gifted can help each other to receive what God has chosen to give, often through the laying on of hands. We see this practice throughout the history of the people of God, especially after the Holy Spirit was given to the church.

1. Moses to Joshua: *"Now Joshua the son of Nun was filled with the spirit of wisdom, for Moses had laid his hands on him; and the sons of Israel listened to him and did as the LORD had commanded Moses"* (Deuteronomy 34:9).

2. The church at Antioch to Barnabas and Paul: *"Then after fasting and praying they laid their hands on them and sent them off"* (Acts 13:3 ESV).

3. The apostles to the seven deacons (Stephen, Philip, etc.): *"They had these men stand before the apostles, who prayed and laid their hands on them"* (Acts 6:6 NRSV).

4. Ananias to Paul: *"So Ananias went and entered the house. He laid his hands on Saul [Paul] and said, 'Brother Saul, the Lord Jesus, who appeared to you on your way here, has sent me so that you may regain your sight and be filled with the Holy Spirit'"* (Acts 9:17 NRSV).

C. Casting a Mantle

The impartation appears to "fall upon" one person from another. Examples include the following:

1. Elijah to Elisha:

    a. In obedience to God, Elijah anointed Elisha as his servant by casting his mantle upon him. (See 1 Kings 19:15–16, 19.)

    b. That simple act determined the course of the rest of Elisha's life. He became Elijah's servant and learned how to operate in God's giftings. Finally, at the end of Elijah's life, Elisha became the sole possessor of the mantle that had once been put over his shoulders (see 2 Kings 2:1–14), and he went on to perform even more miraculous prophetic acts than his mentor, Elijah, had.

2. Jesus to the seventy:

    a. Jesus called His disciples and passed on His authority to them:

        After these things the Lord appointed seventy others also, and sent them two by two before His face into every city and place where He Himself was about to go. Then He said to them, "The harvest truly is great, but the laborers are few; therefore pray the Lord of the harvest to send out laborers into His harvest.... Whatever city you enter, and they receive you, eat such things as are set before you. And heal the sick there, and say to them, 'The kingdom of God has come near to you.'" (Luke 10:1–2, 8–9 NKJV)

b. Jesus' disciples went out without Him and ministered, testing their new gifts; and then they came back to report their successes to Him. *"Then the seventy returned with joy, saying, 'Lord, even the demons are subject to us in Your name'"* (Luke 10:17 NKJV).

IV. SPIRITUAL GIFTS AS FOUND IN SCRIPTURE

A. The following are clearly listed as spiritual gifts. Most of these Scriptures come from four different places in the New Testament where we find gifts listed: Romans 12, 1 Corinthians 12, Ephesians 4, and 1 Peter 4.

1. Administrations, or "steerings" (see 1 Corinthians 12:28)
2. Apostle (see 1 Corinthians 12:28; Ephesians 4:11)
3. Celibacy (see 1 Corinthians 7:7)
4. Discerning (or distinguishing) of spirits (see 1 Corinthians 12:10)
5. Effecting of miracles, or powers (see 1 Corinthians 12:10)
6. Eternal life (see Romans 6:23)
7. Evangelist (see Ephesians 4:11)
8. Exhortation (see Romans 12:8)
9. Faith (see 1 Corinthians 12:9)
10. Giving (see Romans 12:8)
11. Healings (see 1 Corinthians 12:9, 28)
12. Helps (see 1 Corinthians 12:28)
13. Interpretation of tongues (see 1 Corinthians 12:10)
14. Kinds of tongues (see 1 Corinthians 12:10; 1 Corinthians 14:1–34)
15. Leadership, or ruling (see Romans 12:8)
16. Mercy (see Romans 12:8)
17. Pastor, or shepherd (see Ephesians 4:11; Acts 20:28; 1 Peter 5:2)
18. Prophecy (see 1 Corinthians 12:10; 1 Corinthians 14:1)
19. Prophet (see 1 Corinthians 12:28; Ephesians 4:11)
20. Righteousness (see Romans 5:17)
21. Service (see Romans 12:7)
22. Teacher (see 1 Corinthians 12:28; Ephesians 4:11)

23.   Teaching (see Romans 12:7)

24.   Word of knowledge (see 1 Corinthians 12:8)

25.   Word of wisdom (see 1 Corinthians 12:8)

B.   **The following are some other possible spiritual gifts. The scriptural support for such gifts has not been set forth in the form of a list, but it can be seen in biblical anecdotes and in various commands and directives.**

1.   Craftsmanship

2.   Encouragements

3.   Fasting

4.   Hospitality

5.   Intercessory prayer

6.   Interpretation of dreams

7.   Judgment (being a wise judge)

8.   Missions (cross-cultural ministry)

9.   Music

10.   Philanthropy

11.   Worship-leading

V. CLOSING STATEMENTS

A.   A Special Gift Is Given to Each Believer

Every single believer is to have at least one manifestation of the Spirit functioning in his or her life. (See 1 Peter 4:10.) The Lord will identify the gifts and ministries He is giving.

> *But to each one is given the manifestation of the Spirit for the common good. For to one is given the word of wisdom through the Spirit, and to another the word of knowledge according to the same Spirit; to another faith by the same Spirit, and to another gifts of healing by the one Spirit, and to another the effecting of miracles, and to another prophecy, and to another the distinguishing ["discerning" NKJV] of spirits, to another various kinds of tongues, and to another the interpretation of tongues. But one and the same Spirit works all these things, distributing to each one individually just as He wills.*
>
> (1 Corinthians 12:7–11)

B.   Don't Be Ignorant About Your Spiritual Gifts—Learn About Them

> *Now concerning spiritual gifts, brethren, I do not want you to be ignorant…. There are diversities of gifts, but the same Spirit. There are differences of ministries, but the same*

Lord. And there are diversities of activities, but it is the same God who works all in all. (1 Corinthians 12:1, 4–6 NKJV)

As each one has received a special gift, employ it in serving one another as good stewards of the manifold grace of God. (1 Peter 4:10)

C. Do Not Neglect Your Spiritual Gifts

"Do not neglect the spiritual gift within you, which was bestowed on you through prophetic utterance with the laying on of hands by the presbytery" (1 Timothy 4:14). Instead of neglecting your spiritual gifts, stir them up—fan them into flame—for the glory of God. *"Therefore I remind you to stir up the gift of God which is in you through the laying on of my hands"* (2 Timothy 1:6 NKJV).

D. Desire the Gifts of the Holy Spirit

In 1 Corinthians 12:31, Paul wrote, *"But earnestly desire the greater gifts. And I show you a still more excellent way."* Then he went on to extol the supremacy of love in his famous Love Chapter, 1 Corinthians 13. He closed out his discussion of the relationship between spiritual gifts and love by mentioning the importance of pursuing love along with the spiritual gifts: *"Pursue love, yet desire earnestly spiritual gifts"* (1 Corinthians 14:1).

E. Gifts Are Not Given Only to Be Taken Away

Once God gives a gift, He will not withdraw or recall it. *"For the gifts and the calling of God are irrevocable"* (Romans 11:29 NKJV).

F. The Art of Risk-Taking

The gifts are best developed in a climate that endorses "risk-taking and willingness to fail," as John Wimber said. People learn best from a model (such as a spiritual mentor) because they can see and/or hear the gift in operation, and then try it. Then they can think about it and try it again. Eventually, they will "be it" and "do it" for the rest of their lives.

G. The Spirit Is Ready to Release God's Gifts

Since the beginning of time, the Holy Spirit has desired to find people through whom He can manifest Himself. At the time of creation, He "hovered" like a hen over her baby chicks. (See Genesis 1:2.) After the Exodus, Moses said, *"Would that **all** the LORD's people were prophets"* (Numbers 11:29).

The prophet Joel foretold of a day when prophecy, dreams, and visions from God would become widespread:

And it shall come to pass afterward that I will pour out My Spirit on all flesh; your sons and your daughters shall prophesy, your old men shall dream dreams, your young men shall see visions. And also on My menservants and on My maidservants I will pour out My Spirit in those days. (Joel 2:28–29 NKJV)

After Jesus came to earth and the Spirit was given to the church, Peter announced that the day prophesied by Joel had arrived.

> *Peter, standing up with the eleven, raised his voice and said to them, "Men of Judea and all who dwell in Jerusalem, let this be known to you, and heed my words. For these are not drunk, as you suppose, since it is only the third hour of the day. But this is what was spoken by the prophet Joel: 'And it shall come to pass in the last days, says God, that I will pour out of My Spirit on all flesh; your sons and your daughters shall prophesy, your young men shall see visions, your old men shall dream dreams. And on My menservants and on My maidservants I will pour out My Spirit in those days; and they shall prophesy.... And it shall come to pass that whoever calls on the name of the* Lord *shall be saved.'"*   (Acts 2:14–18, 21 NKJV)

Today, we are still living in that day, and God is ministering His gifts to those who will receive them and release them to benefit the church and to raise a dying world to true life.

Questions for Reflection

LESSON ONE:
WHAT ARE THE SPIRITUAL GIFTS?

(Answers to these questions can be found in the back of the study guide.)

Fill in the Blanks

1. In your own words, define the term "spiritual gifts":

    _____

    _____

2. List three purposes of the gifts of the Spirit:

    (a) _____

    (b) _____

    (c) _____

3. Name three ways the gifts of the Spirit are received:

    (a) _____

    (b) _____

    (c) _____

Multiple Choice—Choose the best answer from the list below:

A—good works   C—love

B—manifestation   D—spiritual gifts

4.   *"To each one is given the _____ of the Spirit for the common good"* (1 Corinthians 12:7).

5.   *"Even so you, since you are zealous for _____, let it be for the edification of the church that you seek to excel"* (1 Corinthians 14:12 NKJV).

True or False

6.   Supernatural gifts are needed to reap the great harvest of souls prior to the coming of the Lord.   **T / F**

7.   The gifts are the expression of God's power.   **T / F**

8.   The motive for using the gifts should be to build a ministry.   **T / F**

Scripture Memorization

Write out 1 Corinthians 12:7, 11 and memorize these verses. The following is from the *New American Standard Bible*; choose a different version if you prefer:

To each one is given the manifestation of the Spirit for the common good.... But one and the same Spirit works all these things, distributing to each one individually just as He wills.

Lesson Two

HOW THE HOLY SPIRIT MOVES

"'I will put My Spirit within you and you will come to life, and I will place you on your own land. Then you will know that I, the LORD, have spoken and done it,' declares the LORD."
—Ezekiel 37:14

I. HOW TO RESPOND TO THE HOLY SPIRIT

A. Honor Him as a Guest—*and* Your Landlord

Welcome the Holy Spirit on a first-name basis, yet without overfamiliarity. Acknowledge Him as the third person of the Godhead, with His own distinct personality and ways. As John the Beloved wrote, *"But when He, the Spirit of truth, comes, He will guide you into all the truth; for He will not speak on His own initiative, but whatever He hears, He will speak; and He will disclose to you what is to come"* (John 16:13).

While welcoming the Spirit as a guest, we need to recognize Him also as our Landlord. When we open the door for Him, He's not just making a guest appearance. Don't forget—He *owns* the place!

B. Seek His Presence

The Spirit is more than our special Guest; He is also our Equipper. We must seek to be equipped by Him—continually—so that we can do the work of ministry. He is utterly generous with the gift of Himself, but He wants to be asked. Jesus put it this way:

So I say to you, ask, and it will be given to you; seek, and you will find; knock, and it will be opened to you. For everyone who asks, receives; and he who seeks, finds; and to him who knocks, it will be opened. Now suppose one of you fathers is asked by his son for a

27

fish; he will not give him a snake instead of a fish, will he? Or if he is asked for an egg, he will not give him a scorpion, will he? If you then, being evil, know how to give good gifts to your children, how much more will your heavenly Father give the Holy Spirit to those who ask Him?   (Luke 11:9–13)

The Holy Spirit will not give you a counterfeit gift. And He will never give you too little— or too much. You can never get too filled with Him, because He increases your capacity along the way, opening new rooms in your heart, expanding you to receive more.

C.   Give Him Liberty to Take Charge

Once you have welcomed the Spirit into your innermost being, let Him take charge of you. When you allow Him to have full control, you will find true freedom. You will discover that the Spirit enables you to control the wrongful deeds of your fallen human nature.

Now the Lord is the Spirit, and where the Spirit of the Lord is, there is liberty. But we all, with unveiled face, beholding as in a mirror the glory of the Lord, are being transformed into the same image from glory to glory, just as from the Lord, the Spirit.
                                                                                                   (2 Corinthians 3:17–18)

II. AVOID THESE NEGATIVE RESPONSES

Our ongoing relationship with the Holy Spirit is delicate. It can be damaged all too easily. For this reason, Scripture warns us against a number of attitudes and actions that can disrupt our bond with the Spirit.

A.   Do Not Be Ignorant About the Spirit

Paul reiterated this point at least thirteen times in his epistles, writing, for example, "*Now concerning spiritual gifts, brethren, I do not want you to be ignorant*" (1 Corinthians 12:1 NKJV).

B.   Do Not Grieve the Spirit

Let no unwholesome word proceed from your mouth, but only such a word as is good for edification according to the need of the moment, so that it will give grace to those who hear. Do not grieve the Holy Spirit of God, by whom you were sealed for the day of redemption. Let all bitterness and wrath and anger and clamor and slander be put away from you, along with all malice.   (Ephesians 4:29–31)

One of the most common ways we can grieve the Spirit is by treating our fellow human beings poorly. And when we grieve the Spirit, He subsides. He's still there, but He steps back and waits for us to realize what we've done so that we can repent and repair the damage.

C. Do Not Insult the Presence of the Sensitive Dove of God

Not only is it possible to grieve the Holy Spirit, but it is equally possible to insult Him. When you insult someone, they shut down. They remove themselves from your presence as fast as possible. And they might not come back. The Holy Spirit descended like a dove when Jesus was baptized. (See Matthew 3:16; Mark 1:10; Luke 3:21–22; John 1:32.) Doves are graceful and quiet. They are not self-centered, greedy, or pushy. It doesn't take much to threaten them or to drive them away.

> *How much severer punishment do you think he will deserve who has trampled under foot the Son of God, and has regarded as unclean the blood of the covenant by which he was sanctified, and has insulted the Spirit of grace?*　　　　　　(Hebrews 10:29)

D. Do Not Quench the Spirit

The apostle Paul wrote, *"Do not quench the Spirit"* (1 Thessalonians 5:19). People can quench the Spirit in many ways. Once again, treating others badly can quench the Spirit. Do we cultivate a culture of respect toward others? Do our leaders honor the people under their care, or do they merely tally them as numbers and try to control their behavior? Are husbands and wives treating each other with love and respect? Do they pay attention to scriptural directives for marriage, or do they think they are wiser than the Bible?

E. Do Not Tempt, or Test, the Spirit

Another way of saying this would be, "Do not lie to the Holy Spirit." Dishonest Ananias and his wife, Sapphira, tempted the Spirit when they pretended that the amount of money they were donating to the church was the full amount they had received for a piece of property. (See Acts 5:1–11.) It wouldn't have been wrong for them to have kept some or even all of the money, but it was sinful to make it look like they were more righteous and generous than they were, and their sin cost them their lives. Let us all consider the integrity of our words and our actions, whether we are interacting with people inside or outside of the church.

F. Do Not Blaspheme the Spirit of God

Blasphemy means cursing. Jesus said,

> *Therefore I say to you, any sin and blasphemy shall be forgiven people, but blasphemy against the Spirit shall not be forgiven. Whoever speaks a word against the Son of Man, it shall be forgiven him; but whoever speaks against the Holy Spirit, it shall not be forgiven him, either in this age or in the age to come.*　　　　　(Matthew 12:31–32)

It's one thing to quench or to offend the Holy Spirit, but it's an irreversible sin to utter a curse toward the divine Sustainer of Life, the Spirit of God. The seriousness of the offense against the Spirit depends on the degree of enlightenment a person has achieved.

III. HOW TO MOVE WITH THE HOLY SPIRIT

Walking with the Spirit means walking in the light of God. Some wise person once said that to move in the Holy Spirit means to flow with the Lord so closely as to not cast two shadows.

A. You Must Be Born of the Spirit

The idea of being *"born again"* comes directly from Jesus' discussion with the Pharisee Nicodemus:

> *Jesus answered and said to him, "Truly, truly, I say to you, unless one is born again he cannot see the kingdom of God." Nicodemus said to Him, "How can a man be born when he is old? He cannot enter a second time into his mother's womb and be born, can he?" Jesus answered, "Truly, truly, I say to you, unless one is born of water and the Spirit he cannot enter into the kingdom of God. That which is born of the flesh is flesh, and that which is born of the Spirit is spirit. Do not be amazed that I said to you, 'You must be born again.' The wind blows where it wishes and you hear the sound of it, but do not know where it comes from and where it is going; so is everyone who is born of the Spirit."* (John 3:3–8)

You must be born again first—before you can talk about learning to move with the Spirit. This does not happen by some formula or ritual. The Spirit is involved in our coming to faith initially, and when we hear His invitation, we must open the door of our hearts to Him. In being *"born of the Spirit"* (John 3:6, 8), we give Him permission to do whatever He wants with our lives, and we ask Him to help us walk with Him.

B. You Must Receive and Be Baptized in the Spirit

Jesus said, *"You will receive power when the Holy Spirit has come upon you"* (Acts 1:8).

If you wish to move with the Spirit, you must be baptized with the Spirit. You must allow yourself to be "immersed" in Him. Like being born again, this does not come about through a particular formula. You may or may not feel any "fire" of the Spirit when you are baptized by Him, even though John the Baptist used that term in describing it:

> *As for me, I baptize you with water for repentance, but He who is coming after me is mightier than I, and I am not fit to remove His sandals; He will baptize you with the Holy Spirit and fire.* (Matthew 3:11)

C. You Must Be Continuously Filled with the Spirit

After we are filled with the Spirit, we tend to "leak" as we go through the circumstances of life. We lose track of the Holy Spirit. We grow dull. This does not mean that we need to be baptized in the Spirit over and over again, but we do need to be refilled repeatedly. In the original language of Paul's imperative *"be filled with the Spirit"* (Ephesians 5:18), the verb phrase *"be filled"* is a causative verb in the active voice. It means "go on being filled with the Spirit." A one-time filling will not last. We need to receive more of Him continuously so that we can give to others out of the overflow.

D. You Must Know the Spirit, Hear the Spirit, and See in the Spirit

Knowing the Spirit comes from hearing His whispers and following His voice. Knowing the Spirit enables us to see everything "in the Spirit"—through the Spirit's clear eyes. The Spirit explains things to us. He speaks of new creation realities, and He shows us how to walk in the completed work of Jesus' cross. Jesus knew we would need the Spirit's help when He promised to send Him:

> *I will ask the Father, and He will give you another Helper, that He may be with you forever; that is the Spirit of truth, whom the world cannot receive, because it does not see Him or know Him, but you know Him because He abides with you and will be in you. I will not leave you as orphans; I will come to you.* (John 14:16–18)

E. You Must Hear the Spirit and Not Harden Your Heart

You can have a sustained personal relationship with the Holy Spirit. Pay attention to what He says; do not turn a deaf ear to Him. *"Today, if you hear his voice, do not harden your hearts…"* (Hebrews 3:15 NRSV).

F. You Must Be Led by the Spirit.

> *All who are being led by the Spirit of God, these are sons of God.* (Romans 8:14)

G. You Must Walk in the Spirit

The Holy Spirit comes alongside you to help in every circumstance, because He is your *Paraclete*, your Helper. He is your Friend, your Comforter, the One who gives you strength. *"So I say, walk by the Spirit, and you will not gratify the desires of the flesh [sinful nature]"* (Galatians 5:16 NIV).

H. You Must Pray in the Spirit

"I will pray with the spirit and I will pray with the mind also" (1 Corinthians 14:15). By praying with our spirit in the Holy Spirit (that is, in an unknown tongue furnished by the Spirit), we can catapult beyond our natural understanding. *"But you, beloved, build yourselves up on your most holy faith; pray in the Holy Spirit"* (Jude 1:20 NRSV).

IV. HOW THE SPIRIT MOVES

A. According to the Written Scriptures

The Holy Spirit never moves contrary to the written Word of God. He complements it and does not compete with its instructions and doctrines. We would do well to store up the words of Scripture so that we will have a functioning plumb line in our own spirits. That way, when we think the Spirit is telling us something, we can see if it is in alignment with the Word.

B.   In Agreement with the Father and the Son

There are never any contrary wills in the Godhead. The Holy Spirit reveals the unified counsel of God the Father and God the Son.

C.   The Spirit Makes Jesus Real to Us

The Spirit reveals Jesus as a living reality and brings us into a deeper relationship with Him in an ongoing way. Jesus introduces us to the Father, just as He said: *"I am the way, and the truth, and the life; no one comes to the Father but through Me"* (John 14:6). And as Jesus reveals the Father, the Holy Spirit reveals Jesus. It's an interdependent cycle, and we are privileged to participate in it.

D.   The Spirit Is Our Life-Giving Source

The Spirit is the One who brings us into the life of the Lord Jesus. He makes true disciples of us, because He is interested in maturing our character more than in bringing us personal comfort. He brings us truth, not false assurance or false comfort. He convicts, persuades, shepherds, and leads us to the life-source of God.

E.   The Spirit Enables Us to Witness and to Pray

The Spirit helps us to overcome our fears, and He stretches us beyond ourselves, moving us to testify of the love and power of God and showing us how to bear fruit that lasts. (See John 15:16.) The Spirit always knows exactly what God wants to do in our lives. That's why praying in the Spirit is so effective:

> *In the same way the Spirit also helps our weakness; for we do not know how to pray as we should, but the Spirit Himself intercedes for us with groanings too deep for words; and He who searches the hearts knows what the mind of the Spirit is, because He intercedes for the saints according to the will of God.* (Romans 8:26–27)

V. OPEN YOURSELF TO THE SPIRIT

A.   Quiet Yourself Before the Lord

Avoid hurrying. Instead, get your spirit's tank refilled with the Holy Spirit. It is best to establish a pattern of doing it the first thing in the morning so that you can return to that inner place of peace and trust anytime throughout the day, finding your satisfaction in Him. The psalmist compared a quieted soul to a contented young child who has been well cared for, whose hunger has been fully satisfied: *"My soul is like a weaned child within me"* (Psalm 131:2).

> *I wait for the Lord, my soul does wait, and in His word do I hope. My soul waits for the Lord more than the watchmen for the morning; indeed, more than the watchmen for the morning.* (Psalm 130:5–6)

B. Pray in the Spirit

Throughout the day, exercise the gift of tongues; pray in the Spirit. This will build your faith very effectively and turn you toward the Father's heart. Paul wrote, *"I speak in tongues more than you all"* (1 Corinthians 14:18), and what he meant was that he relied heavily on this gift.

C. Determine to Get Involved

Make a conscious determination to be a participant in whatever the Holy Spirit wants to do, instead of remaining merely a passive observer. When you go to worship meetings, be ready to get involved, eager to give and not only to receive. At the minimum, you should be an intercessor, praying for those who are leading the meeting.

D. Realize That God Wants to Use You

Even if you are having a proverbial "bad day," you still have something alive within you that you can give away, something the world does not have—the hope of glory. When you walk and move in the strength and counsel that the Spirit supplies, you operate in God's grace.

E. Acknowledge That It Is Only by Grace

Ask the Holy Spirit for a fresh revelation of God's grace. You already know that you cannot earn the gifts of the Spirit or access the power of God without grace. When you move with the Spirit in God's grace, all the credit and all the glory returns to God, where it belongs.

VI. VARIETIES OF RELEASES

A. Varieties of Gifts

> *Now there are varieties of gifts, but the same Spirit.*   (1 Corinthians 12:4, ESV)

B. Varieties of Ministries

> *And there are varieties of service ["ministries" NASB], but the same Lord.*
> (1 Corinthians 12:5 ESV)

C. Varieties of Activities

> *And there are varieties of activities, but it is the same God who empowers them all in everyone.*   (1 Corinthians 12:6 ESV)

LESSON TWO:
HOW THE HOLY SPIRIT MOVES

(Answers to these questions can be found in the back of the study guide.)

Fill in the Blank

1.   One definition of moving in the Holy Spirit is to so flow with the Lord as to not cast two

   _____.

2.   *"So I say to you, _____, and it will be _____ to you; seek, and you will find; knock, and it will be opened to you. For everyone who asks, receives; and he who seeks, finds; and to him who knocks, it will be opened. Now suppose one of you fathers is asked by his son for a fish; he will not give him a snake instead of a fish, will he? Or if he is asked for an egg, he will not give him a scorpion, will he? If you then, being evil, know how to give good gifts to your children, how much more will your heavenly Father give the Holy Spirit to those who ask Him?"* (Luke 11:9–13).

3.   *"So I say, _____ by the Spirit, and you will not gratify the desires of the flesh [sinful nature]"* (Galatians 5:16 NIV).

Multiple Choice—Choose the best answer from the list below:

   A—grace   C—kingdom
   B—heart   D—gratitude

4.   The Holy Spirit ushers us into the _____ of God.

5.   You cannot earn the gifts of the Spirit or access the power of God without the _____ of God.

True or False

6.   The Holy Spirit seldom moves contrary to the Word of God.   **T / F**

7.   Being baptized and filled with the Spirit guarantees lifelong joy, power, and faith.   **T / F**

8.   The Holy Spirit is always in agreement with the Father and the Son.   **T / F**

Scripture Memorization

Write out John 14:16–18 and memorize it. The following is from the *New King James Version*; choose another version if you prefer:

> *I will pray the Father, and He will give you another Helper, that He may abide with you forever—the Spirit of truth, whom the world cannot receive, because it neither sees Him nor knows Him; but you know Him, for He dwells with you and will be in you. I will not leave you orphans; I will come to you.*

HOW TO GROW IN EXERCISING SPIRITUAL GIFTS

"Follow the way of love and eagerly desire gifts of the Spirit…. Since you are eager for gifts of the Spirit, try to excel in those that build up the church…. When you come together, each of you has a hymn, or a word of instruction, a revelation, a tongue or an interpretation. Everything must be done so that the church may be built up."
—1 Corinthians 14:1, 12, 26 (NIV)

I. PRACTICAL BIBLICAL FOUNDATIONS

A. Gifts Thrive in the Context of a Believing Fellowship

> *I will not leave you as orphans; I will come to you.*　　　　　(John 14:18 NIV)

If Jesus had not fulfilled the above promise, enabling us to be adopted into the heavenly family of His Father God, you and I would be orphans—having no spiritual position and being unable to provide for ourselves. But He did follow through, and we are God's adopted sons and daughters.

Jesus welcomed us into His family by giving us gifts, which have been set solely within the framework of a fellowship of believers—the body of Christ—in an atmosphere of expectant faith, worship, and waiting upon Him:

> *For by one Spirit we were all baptized into one body,…and we were all made to drink of one Spirit.*　　　　　(1 Corinthians 12:13)

36

God shines His brilliant light through the gifts. He illuminates our innermost beings (see Proverbs 20:27), and He shows His glory to the world at large. Jesus said,

> *You are the light of the world. A city set on a hill cannot be hidden; nor does anyone light a lamp and put it under a basket, but on the lampstand, and it gives light to all who are in the house.* (Matthew 5:14–15)

The spiritual gifts are not given to isolated individuals because, by definition, anybody who has been adopted into the family of God is no longer alone. We are not orphans, and none of us is an only child, either. Spiritual gifts are given only within a community setting, and they shine forth with collective brightness.

B. We Need Others' Gifts

No one can exercise their spiritual gifts in isolation, apart from other people. We need each other's ministry. We need each other's encouragement in the faith. And we flourish within a culture where believers are *"devoted to one another in brotherly love; [giving] preference to one another in honor"* (Romans 12:10).

An assembly of believers is like a human body, with each member having a specific function. We find safety and accountability there, and in truth our gifts cannot work as they were intended outside of the body.

C. Our Gifts Must Be Used Actively

We cannot be passive, hoping that the Spirit will move us in some way. We need to stir ourselves up. Jesus told us to *go*:

> *And He said to [His disciples], "Go into all the world and preach the gospel to all creation.... These signs will accompany those who have believed: in My name they will cast out demons, they will speak with new tongues; they will pick up serpents, and if they drink any deadly poison, it will not hurt them; they will lay hands on the sick, and they will recover."... And they went out and preached everywhere, while the Lord worked with them, and confirmed the word by the signs that followed.* (Mark 16:15, 17–18, 20)

Signs follow believers who go. God waits for His people to go forth so that He might demonstrate the power of the cross of Christ and impart life to the spiritually hungry. Signs confirm the truth—for believers and nonbelievers alike.

D. We Must Continually Follow the Spirit

God distributes gifts according to His will.

> *All these are empowered by one and the same Spirit, who apportions to each one individually as he wills.* (1 Corinthians 12:11 ESV)

God added his testimony by signs and wonders and various miracles, and by gifts of the Holy Spirit, distributed according to his will.   (Hebrews 2:4 NRSV)

1. The New Testament keeps telling us to ask and receive because, as we earnestly seek God, He changes the desires of our hearts to match His; our requests line up with His will, and we end up asking for exactly what He knows we need.

    As former orphans, we can rejoice in the new life God has given us: *"For all who are being led by the Spirit of God, these are sons of God"* (Romans 8:14).

2. Certain gifts are always within the will of God to ask for in prayer, such as the gifts of prophecy, tongues, and interpretation of tongues. (See 1 Corinthians 14:1, 5, 13.) Move out in faith today, stirring up your gift and asking God for more.

E. Trust God's Wisdom as You Ask and Receive

1. *If you then, being evil, know how to give good gifts to your children, how much more will your heavenly Father give the Holy Spirit to those who ask Him?*
                                        (Luke 11:13; see also Matthew 7:11)

2. *Therefore I say to you, all things for which you pray and ask, believe that you have received them, and they will be granted you.*   (Mark 11:24)

F. Practice Makes Perfect

You learn correct, mature exercise of the gifts as you use them:

1. *For you can all prophesy one by one, so that all may learn and all be encouraged.*
                                        (1 Corinthians 14:31 ESV)

2. *But solid food belongs to those who are of full age, that is, those who by reason of use have their senses exercised to discern both good and evil.*   (Hebrews 5:14 NKJV)

G. Check Your Motives

Always use your gifts for the sake of the people around you:

So also you, since you are zealous of spiritual gifts, seek to abound for the edification of the church.   (1 Corinthians 14:12)

Never let your exercise of a gift become a performance, especially if your gift puts you on the platform in front of others. You are not building your own little kingdom; rather, you have been adopted into God's family, making you a citizen of *His* kingdom!

II. CREATIVE HOLY SPIRIT

The Holy Spirit expresses Himself through an endless variety of spiritual gifts, ministries, and operations within the body of Christ.

Now there are varieties of gifts, but the same Spirit; and there are varieties of service ["ministries" NASB], but the same Lord; and there are varieties of activities, but it is the same God who empowers them all in everyone. (1 Corinthians 12:4–6 ESV)

A. No Single "Right" Way

Ministries are made up of a collection of gifts; and the wide variety of gifts, expressed through different personalities, is further varied by the surrounding circumstances and culture.

B. One God, Many Expressions

Despite the great variety of expressions, everything stems from the same God. The same Holy Spirit expresses His grace in a distinct manner each time He is allowed to work in and through somebody. He does not limit Himself to working through "religious professionals" or even to a particular polished mode of expression. Our Creator's life flows through any member of His body who says "yes" to Him.

III. SCRIPTURES TO BUILD YOUR FAITH

Read through these Scriptures—they will help to build your faith for the exercise of your spiritual gifts.

A. The Exercise of Spiritual Gifts Brings Glory to God

As each one has received a special gift, employ it in serving one another as good stewards of the manifold grace of God. Whoever speaks, is to do so as one who is speaking the utterances of God; whoever serves is to do so as one who is serving by the strength which God supplies; so that in all things God may be glorified through Jesus Christ, to whom belongs the glory and dominion forever and ever. Amen. (1 Peter 4:10–11)

B. The Exercise of Spiritual Gifts Edifies and Builds Up Others

Those who speak in a tongue build up themselves, but those who prophesy build up the church. Now I would like all of you to speak in tongues, but even more to prophesy. One who prophesies is greater than one who speaks in tongues, unless someone interprets, so that the church may be built up.... So with yourselves; since you are eager for spiritual gifts, strive to excel in them for building up the church.
(1 Corinthians 14:4–5, 12 NRSV)

C. God Wants Every Believer to Exercise Spiritual Gifts

Whenever God wants to bring His kingdom to bear on something, His first choice is to use a spiritual-gift-equipped follower. Again, that man or woman or child does not have to be a "professional religious person"; God typically uses the nearest available believer to accomplish His purposes throughout the world.

> *To each one is given the manifestation of the Spirit for the common good.... But one and the same Spirit works all these things, distributing to each one individually just as He wills.*
>
> (1 Corinthians 12:7, 11)

> *When you assemble, each one has a psalm, has a teaching, has a revelation, has a tongue, has an interpretation. Let all things be done for edification.*
>
> (1 Corinthians 14:26)

D.   Spiritual Gifts Are Tools, Not Toys

The gifts are channels for God's love. Believers need to practice using them, understanding that nobody will be an expert on his or her first try. It feels risky to step out in public to use them, and one really does have to be willing to appear stupid and to fail. Nothing is guaranteed, except that the Holy Spirit will be with you and will help you.

> *But earnestly desire the greater gifts. And I show you a still more excellent way.... Pursue love, yet desire earnestly spiritual gifts, but especially that you may prophesy.*
>
> (1 Corinthians 12:31; 14:1)

E.   God Will Faithfully Give His Gifts to Us, and if We Love Him, We Will Desire to Receive and Exercise Them

> *If you then, being evil, know how to give good gifts to your children, how much more will your heavenly Father give the Holy Spirit to those who ask Him?*
>
> (Luke 11:13; see also Matthew 7:11)

> *Do not be deceived, my beloved brethren. Every good thing given and every perfect gift is from above, coming down from the Father of lights, with whom there is no variation or shifting shadow.*
>
> (James 1:16–17)

F.   Spiritual Gifts Will Continue to Operate Until Christ Comes Again

> *I give thanks to my God always for you because of the grace of God that was given you in Christ Jesus, that in every way you were enriched in him in all speech and all knowledge—even as the testimony about Christ was confirmed among you—so that you are not lacking in any gift, as you wait for the revealing of our Lord Jesus Christ, who will sustain you to the end, guiltless in the day of our Lord Jesus Christ.*
>
> (1 Corinthians 1:4–8 ESV)

> *And it shall come to pass in the last days, says God, that I will pour out of My Spirit on all flesh; your sons and your daughters shall prophesy, your young men shall see visions,*

*your old men shall dream dreams. And on My menservants and on My maidservants I will pour out My Spirit in those days; and they shall prophesy. I will show wonders in heaven above and signs in the earth beneath: blood and fire and vapor of smoke. The sun shall be turned into darkness, and the moon into blood, before the coming of the great and awesome day of the L*ORD*.*   (Acts 2:17–20 NKJV)

G. Just as the Apostles Needed Supernatural Power in Their Ministry in the First Century, so Do We:

You shall receive power when the Holy Spirit has come upon you; and you shall be witnesses to Me in Jerusalem, and in all Judea and Samaria, and to the end of the earth.
                                                                            (Acts 1:8 NKJV)

When Peter saw this, he replied to the people, "Men of Israel, why are you amazed at this, or why do you gaze at us, as if by our own power or piety we had made him walk?"   (Acts 3:12)

And with great power the apostles gave witness to the resurrection of the Lord Jesus. And great grace was upon them all.   (Acts 4:33 NKJV)

And my God will supply all your needs according to His riches in glory in Christ Jesus.   (Philippians 4:19)

H. God Ordained That the Gospel Should be Preached with Signs Following

And [Jesus] said to them, "Go into all the world and preach the gospel to all creation. He who has believed and has been baptized shall be saved; but he who has disbelieved shall be condemned. These signs will accompany those who have believed: in My name they will cast out demons, they will speak with new tongues; they will pick up serpents, and if they drink any deadly poison, it will not hurt them; they will lay hands on the sick, and they will recover." So then, when the Lord Jesus had spoken to them, He was received up into heaven and sat down at the right hand of God. And they went out and preached everywhere, while the Lord worked with them, and confirmed the word by the signs that followed.   (Mark 16:15–20)

Philip went down to the city of Samaria and proclaimed to them the Christ. And the crowds with one accord paid attention to what was being said by Philip when they heard him and saw the signs that he did. For unclean spirits, crying out with a loud voice, came out of many who had them, and many who were paralyzed or lame were healed.
                                                                            (Acts 8:5–7 ESV)

When Paul had gathered a bundle of sticks and put them on the fire, a viper came out because of the heat and fastened on his hand. When the native people saw the creature hanging from his hand, they said to one another, "No doubt this man is a murderer. Though he has escaped from the sea, Justice has not allowed him to live." He, however, shook off the creature into the fire and suffered no harm. They were waiting for him to swell up or suddenly fall down dead. But when they had waited a long time and saw no misfortune come to him, they changed their minds and said that he was a god. Now in the neighborhood of that place were lands belonging to the chief man of the island, named Publius, who received us and entertained us hospitably for three days. It happened that the father of Publius lay sick with fever and dysentery. And Paul visited him and prayed, and putting his hands on him healed him. And when this had taken place, the rest of the people on the island who had diseases also came and were cured. They also honored us greatly, and when we were about to sail, they put on board whatever we needed.

(Acts 28:3–10 ESV)

For I will not venture to speak of anything except what Christ has accomplished through me to win obedience from the Gentiles, by word and deed, by the power of signs and wonders, by the power of the Spirit of God, so that from Jerusalem and as far around as Illyricum I have fully proclaimed the good news of Christ. (Romans 15:18–19 NRSV)

Therefore we must pay greater attention to what we have heard, so that we do not drift away from it. For if the message declared through angels was valid, and every transgression or disobedience received a just penalty, how can we escape if we neglect so great a salvation? It was declared at first through the Lord, and it was attested to us by those who heard him, while God added his testimony by signs and wonders and various miracles, and by gifts of the Holy Spirit, distributed according to his will.

(Hebrews 2:1–4 NRSV)

There are more "heathen" in the world today who have not heard the gospel than there were in the days of the apostles! Therefore, we should expect unprecedented displays of God's grace and supernatural power to testify to the resurrection of Jesus Christ and to give glory to God the Father.

The church (which is made up of individuals like you and me) needs to stir up and exercise the gifts of the Holy Spirit more than ever before. This is not the time to settle into a comfortable resting mode; it is the time to shed every encumbrance and to obey these words of Jesus:

All authority has been given to Me in heaven and on earth. Go therefore and make disciples of all the nations, baptizing them in the name of the Father and of the Son and of the Holy Spirit, teaching them to observe all things that I have commanded you; and lo, I am with you always, even to the end of the age. Amen.

(Matthew 28:18–20 NKJV)

Questions for Reflection

LESSON THREE:
HOW TO GROW IN EXERCISING SPIRITUAL GIFTS

(Answers to these questions can be found in the back of the study guide.)

Fill in the Blank

1.   The exercise of spiritual gifts brings glory to _____.

2.   *"As each one has received a _____ _____, employ it in serving one another as good stewards of the manifold grace of God"* (1 Peter 4:10).

3.   *"So also you, since you are zealous of spiritual gifts, seek to abound for the _____ of the church"* (1 Corinthians 14:12).

Multiple Choice—Choose the best answer from the list below:

A—community   C—emphasis

B—distribution   D—caring

4.   The _____ of gifts is according to God's will.

5.   Spiritual gifts are given only within a _____ setting.

True or False

6.   Spiritual gifts are channels through which love flows.   **T / F**

7.   Gifts will continue in operation until Christ comes.   **T / F**

8.   The exercise of gifts brings glory to God.   **T / F**

Scripture Memorization

Write out 1 Peter 4:10–11 and memorize it. The following is from the *New Revised Standard Version*; choose a different version if you prefer.

Like good stewards of the manifold grace of God, serve one another with whatever gift each of you has received. Whoever speaks must do so as one speaking the very words of God; whoever serves must do so with the strength that God supplies, so that God may be glorified in all things through Jesus Christ. To him belong the glory and the power forever and ever. Amen.

REVELATORY GIFTS—THE GIFTS THAT REVEAL

"[May] the God of our Lord Jesus Christ, the Father of glory…give to you a spirit of wisdom and of revelation in the knowledge of Him."
—Ephesians 1:17

The gifts of discerning of spirits, a word of wisdom, and a word of knowledge have *revelation* in common—through them, God uncovers hidden motives and information that can be used to bring liberty from spiritual bondage and to enable effective outreach. Through the use of these gifts, we can better cooperate with the invisible movements of the Holy Spirit.

THE GIFT OF DISCERNING OF SPIRITS

"Beloved, do not believe every spirit, but test the spirits to see whether they are from God."
—1 John 4:1

I. THE GIFT OF DISCERNING OF SPIRITS DEFINED

People who have the gift of *"discerning of spirits"* (1 Corinthians 12:10 NKJV) can perceive both good and evil spirits in the unseen world and differentiate between them. *"Discerning of spirits"* is also called *"distinguishing of spirits"* (NASB), *"the ability to distinguish between spirits"* (ESV), and *"discernment of spirits"* (NRSV).

We can best define the gift of discerning of spirits by exploring it from various angles. Here is how several Bible teachers (listed below in alphabetical order by their last names) have defined this gift:

A. Kenneth Hagin (late father of the Word of Faith movement)

"To discern" means *to perceive by seeing or hearing....*

This gift has to do with the entire class of spirits, including good spirits, bad spirits, and human spirits. It is supernatural insight into the realm of *spirits.*

...[It] deals with three classes of spirits: divine, satanic, and human. So you see, discerning of spirits may be discerning [even] the similitude of God.[1]

B. Dick Iverson (author, founding pastor of City Bible Church [Oregon], formerly called Portland Bible Temple)

The gift of discerning spirits is the God-given ability or enablement to recognize the identity (and very often the personality and condition) of the spirits which are behind different manifestations or activities.

To discern means to perceive, distinguish or differentiate. The dividing line between a human and divine operation may be obscure to some believers, but one with the faculty of spiritual discernment sees a clear separation.[2]

C. Derek Prince (late author, international Bible teacher)

As Derek Prince explained, discerning of spirits is the supernatural ability to recognize and distinguish between not only good and bad spirits but also various classes of spirits:

1. the Holy Spirit
2. good angels
3. fallen angels
4. demons or evil spirits
5. the human spirit[3]

While knowledge is the impartation of a fact, discernment is a form of direct perception.[4]

D. David Pytches (Anglican bishop, author)

[The gift of discerning of spirits] is a supernatural gift of perception given sovereignly by God to enable individuals in the church to distinguish the motivating spirit behind certain words or deeds.[5]

E. Sam Storms (author, Bible teacher, former visiting associate professor of theology at Wheaton College)

This spiritual gift may be the ability to pass discerning judgment on prophetic utterances, thereby standing in relation to the gift of prophecy the way interpretation does to the gift of tongues (see 1 Cor. 14:29).

...But the spiritual gift of distinguishing of spirits is probably a supernaturally enabled sense or feeling concerning the nature and source of the spirit.[6]

F. Peter Wagner (missiologist, author, apostolic teacher)

The gift of discerning of spirits (or discernment) is the special ability that God gives to certain members of the body of Christ to know with assurance whether certain behaviors purported to be of God are in reality divine, human or satanic (Matthew 16:21–23; Acts 5:1–11; 16:16–18; 1 Corinthians 12:10; 1 John 4:1–6).[7]

G.   John Wimber (late author, international Vineyard leader)

Discerning of spirits is the supernatural capacity to judge whether the spirit operating has a source that is human, demonic, or divine. It is a supernatural perception in the spiritual realm for the purpose of determining the source of spiritual activity.[8]

II. EXAMPLES OF DISCERNING OF SPIRITS

Each believer is endowed with a different level of expertise in each of the categories of discernment.

A.   Discerning the Holy Spirit

1.   John the Baptist discerned the Holy Spirit when the Spirit descended upon Jesus from heaven like a dove at His baptism:

> *John testified saying, "I have seen the Spirit descending as a dove out of heaven, and He remained upon Him. I did not recognize Him, but He who sent me to baptize in water said to me, 'He upon whom you see the Spirit descending and remaining upon Him, this is the One who baptizes in the Holy Spirit.'"*   (John 1:32–33)

2.   The believers in the upper room on the day of Pentecost discerned the presence of the Holy Spirit as the sound of rushing wind and then as tongues of fire resting on their heads. We don't know if they could discern these things with their natural eyes and ears or if it was entirely supernatural, but in any case, they agreed on what they had experienced.

> *When the Day of Pentecost had fully come, they were all with one accord in one place. And suddenly there came a sound from heaven, as of a rushing mighty wind, and it filled the whole house where they were sitting. Then there appeared to them divided tongues, as of fire, and one sat upon each of them. And they were all filled with the Holy Spirit and began to speak with other tongues, as the Spirit gave them utterance.*   (Acts 2:1–4 NKJV)

B.   Discerning Angels

1.   An angel appeared to Jesus in the garden of Gethsemane: *"Then an angel appeared to Him from heaven, strengthening Him"* (Luke 22:43 NKJV).

2.   Mary saw two angels in the sepulcher where Jesus' body had been laid:

> *But Mary stood outside by the tomb weeping, and as she wept she stooped down and looked into the tomb. And she saw two angels in white sitting, one at the head and the other at the feet, where the body of Jesus had lain. Then they said to her, "Woman, why are you weeping?" She said to them, "Because they have taken away my Lord, and I do not know where they have laid Him."*   (John 20:11–13 NKJV)

3.   An angel appeared to Paul to give him a message of reassurance during a violent storm at sea.

> *Since they had been without food for a long time, Paul then stood up among them and said, "Men, you should have listened to me and not have set sail from Crete and thereby avoided this damage and loss. I urge you now to keep up your courage, for there will be no loss of life among you, but only of the ship. For last night there stood by me an angel of the God to whom I belong and whom I worship, and he said, 'Do not be afraid, Paul; you must stand before the emperor; and indeed, God has granted safety to all those who are sailing with you.'"*   (Acts 27:21–24 NRSV)

C.   Discerning Human Spirits

1.   Jesus discerned a guileless spirit in Nathanael:

> *Jesus saw Nathanael coming toward Him, and said of him, "Behold, an Israelite indeed, in whom is no deceit!"*   (John 1:47 NKJV)

2.   Jesus often discerned sinful motives in human spirits:

> *But Jesus, on His part, was not entrusting Himself to them, for He knew all men, and because He did not need anyone to testify concerning man, for He Himself knew what was in man.*   (John 2:24–25)

3.   Peter discerned the wrong motives of Simon the magician:

> *Peter said to him, "May your silver perish with you, because you thought you could obtain the gift of God with money! You have no part or portion in this matter, for your heart is not right before God. Therefore repent of this wickedness of yours, and pray the Lord that, if possible, the intention of your heart may be forgiven you. For I see that you are in the gall of bitterness and in the bondage of iniquity." But Simon answered and said, "Pray to the Lord for me yourselves, so that nothing of what you have said may come upon me."*   (Acts 8:20–24)

4.   Paul discerned a "spirit of faith" in a lame man. (See also 2 Corinthians 4:13.)

> *At Lystra a man was sitting who had no strength in his feet, lame from his mother's womb, who had never walked. This man was listening to Paul as*

> *he spoke, who, when he had fixed his gaze on him and had seen that he had faith to be made well, said with a loud voice, "Stand upright on your feet." And he leaped up and began to walk.* (Acts 14:8–10)

D. Discerning Evil Spirits

1. Jesus discerned a spirit of infirmity that was causing a woman to have severe curvature of the spine:

   > *There was a woman who for eighteen years had had a sickness caused by a spirit; and she was bent double, and could not straighten up at all. When Jesus saw her, He called her over and said to her, "Woman, you are freed from your sickness." And He laid His hands on her; and immediately she was made erect again and began glorifying God.* (Luke 13:11–13)

2. Paul discerned a spirit of divination (named "Python" in the Greek) operating through a slave girl in Philippi:

   > *It happened that as we were going to the place of prayer, a slave-girl having a spirit of divination met us, who was bringing her masters much profit by fortune-telling. Following after Paul and us, she kept crying out, saying, "These men are bond-servants of the Most High God, who are proclaiming to you the way of salvation." She continued doing this for many days. But Paul was greatly annoyed, and turned and said to the spirit, "I command you in the name of Jesus Christ to come out of her!" And it came out at that very moment.* (Acts 16:16–18)

3. John saw three unclean spirits that looked like frogs:

   > *And I saw, coming out of the mouth of the dragon and out of the mouth of the beast and out of the mouth of the false prophet, three unclean spirits like frogs. For they are demonic spirits, performing signs....* (Revelation 16:13–14 ESV)

III. PURPOSE OF THE GIFT

A. To Deliver People from Demons

One of the primary purposes of the gift of discerning of spirits is for the sake of people's *deliverance*. This is what we see when Jesus encountered the Gerasene demoniac. (See Mark 5:1–20.) Jesus arrived in the region, discerned and cast out the *"legion"* of demons in the man, and then went away. He didn't stay to preach or work miracles. Deliverance of that one man was the entire purpose of Jesus' visit. (See also, for example, Acts 8:5–7.)

B.   To Reveal and Expose the Servants of Satan

A related purpose of this gift is to reveal and expose the servants of Satan and to put a halt to their work and utterances.

1.   This is what happened when Paul exposed the evil motives of Elymas the magician: *"Saul, who was also known as Paul, filled with the Holy Spirit, fixed his gaze on him, and said, 'You who are full of all deceit and fraud, you son of the devil, you enemy of all righteousness, will you not cease to make crooked the straight ways of the Lord?'"* (Acts 13:9–10).

2.   In Philippi, after Paul had discerned and cast out the evil spirit from the slave girl, not only did evangelism take root in the region, but the slave girl's owners could no longer exploit her demonic gift for financial gain. (See Acts 16:16–40.)

C.   To Expose Error

The gift of discerning of spirits is a vital help in exposing false prophets and satanic error in doctrine. Paul wrote, *"The Spirit explicitly says that in later times some will fall away from the faith, paying attention to deceitful spirits and doctrines of demons, by means of the hypocrisy of liars seared in their own conscience as with a branding iron"* (1 Timothy 4:1–2).

John provided a useful test for verifying discernment; you could call it the "Jesus is Lord" test. A fallen angel or demonic spirit simply does not have the ability to state the truth that Jesus Christ has come in the flesh as the Son of God:

> *Beloved, do not believe every spirit, but test the spirits to see whether they are from God, because many false prophets have gone out into the world. By this you know the Spirit of God: every spirit that confesses that Jesus Christ has come in the flesh is from God; and every spirit that does not confess Jesus is not from God; this is the spirit of the antichrist, of which you have heard that it is coming, and now it is already in the world.... We are from God; he who knows God listens to us; he who is not from God does not listen to us. By this we know the spirit of truth and the spirit of error.*   (1 John 4:1–3, 6)

D.   To Acknowledge and Confess Christ

> *No one speaking by the Spirit of God says, "Jesus is accursed"; and no one can say, "Jesus is Lord," except by the Holy Spirit.*
>
>   (1 Corinthians 12:3; see also Matthew 13:13–17)

E.   To Know the Moving of the Holy Spirit so as to Cooperate with Him

The underlying purpose of the gift of discerning of spirits is so that a person can follow the moving of the Holy Spirit. By the operation of this gift, a person can better cooperate with the Spirit, whose movements are often so discreet as to be almost imperceptible. The Scriptures describe the Holy Spirit as being like the wind: *"The wind blows where it wishes and you hear the sound of it, but do not know where it comes from and where it is going; so is everyone who is born of the Spirit"* (John 3:8; see also Ezekiel 37:9–10).

IV. GUIDELINES FOR OPERATING IN THE GIFT OF DISCERNING OF SPIRITS

A. Cultivate the Gift

The gift of discerning of spirits can be cultivated. Your senses can be trained, and over time you can learn from experience how to interpret what your senses pick up. Scripture says, *"Solid food is for the mature, who because of practice have their senses trained to discern good and evil"* (Hebrews 5:14).

B. Immerse Yourself in God's Word

Immerse yourself in the Word so that you can recall key truths, as needed, to confirm your senses.

C. Test the Spirits

Remember the "Jesus is Lord" test. (See 1 John 4:1–3, 6.)

D. Examine the Fruit

Sometimes, the clearest way to understand your discernment is to examine the fruit of a person's life. Jesus said,

> *You will know them by their fruits. Grapes are not gathered from thorn bushes nor figs from thistles, are they? So every good tree bears good fruit, but the bad tree bears bad fruit. A good tree cannot produce bad fruit, nor can a bad tree produce good fruit. Every tree that does not bear good fruit is cut down and thrown into the fire. So then, you will know them by their fruits.* (Matthew 7:16–20)

E. Recognize That the Gift of Discerning of Spirits Is Not the "Gift of Suspicion"

Examine the fruit within your own life, too. The gift of discerning of spirits is not the "gift of suspicion." Your insights and perceptions should never be used in gossip or for purposes of defamation, but always for edification and building up the body of Christ. The Holy Spirit wants to heal and restore the members of the body, not harm them. Never ally yourself with the accuser of the brethren, the devil! (See Revelation 12:10.) Paul addressed this point:

> *I therefore, the prisoner in the Lord, beg you to lead a life worthy of the calling to which you have been called, with all humility and gentleness, with patience, bearing with one another in love, making every effort to maintain the unity of the Spirit in the bond of*

peace. There is one body and one Spirit, just as you were called to the one hope of your calling, one Lord, one faith, one baptism, one God and Father of all, who is above all and through all and in all.... Put away from you all bitterness and wrath and anger and wrangling and slander, together with all malice, and be kind to one another, tenderhearted, forgiving one another, as God in Christ has forgiven you.

(Ephesians 4:1–6, 31–32 NRSV)

F. Ask God to Supply You with Wisdom

Wisdom is crucial to the exercise of the gift of discerning of spirits. This gift can be explosive. To keep from learning everything the hard way (and potentially doing damage along the way), obtain wisdom beyond your years by consulting others who have greater experience with the gift. And remember that the greatest ally of wisdom is love.

G. Intercede

Ask for extra faith to act or to pray with authority. Get into the habit of praying a discernment or a revelation back to the Father before you act on it. Seek His guidance for the application of what you have received. Even if He does not want you to step out and say something or act in a particular way, you can always intercede in prayer; Spirit-guided intercession is always appropriate. If He seems to give you the go-ahead, you may release a command to rebuke an enemy you have discerned.

God will guide you all along the way; just keep up an ongoing conversation with Him. With the apostle Peter, I say to you, *"Grace and peace be multiplied to you in the knowledge of God and of Jesus our Lord; seeing that His divine power has granted to us everything pertaining to life and godliness"* (2 Peter 1:2–3).

LESSON FOUR: THE GIFT OF DISCERNING OF SPIRITS

(Answers to these questions can be found in the back of the study guide.)

Fill in the Blank

1. *"By this you know the Spirit of God: every spirit that confesses that _____ _____ has come in the flesh is from God"* (1 John 4:2).

2. In your own words, define the gift of discerning of spirits: _____

    _____

    _____

    _____

3. List four areas of discernment that one may operate in:

    (a) _____

    (b) _____

    (c) _____

    (d) _____

Multiple Choice—Choose the best answer from the list below:

A—acknowledge   C—know

B—expose   D—cultivate

4.   One purpose of the gift of discerning of spirits is to _____ the works of Satan.

5.   Another purpose of the gift of discerning of spirits is to _____ the moving of the Holy Spirit.

True or False

6.   The gift of discerning of spirits gives a person the capacity to judge whether the spirit operating has a source that is human, demonic, or divine.   **T / F**

7.   You can cultivate the gift of discerning of spirits by exercising your spiritual senses.   **T / F**

8.   The gift of discerning of spirits is the "gift of suspicion."   **T / F**

Scripture Memorization

Write out 1 John 4:1–3, 6 and memorize it. This is from the *New American Standard Version*; choose a different Bible translation if you prefer:

Beloved, do not believe every spirit, but test the spirits to see whether they are from God, because many false prophets have gone out into the world. By this you know the Spirit of God: every spirit that confesses that Jesus Christ has come in the flesh is from God; and every spirit that does not confess Jesus is not from God; this is the spirit of the antichrist, of which you have heard that it is coming, and now it is already in the world.... By this we know the spirit of truth and the spirit of error.

Lesson Five

THE GIFT OF A
WORD OF WISDOM

> *"Yet among the mature we do impart wisdom, although it is not a wisdom of this age or of the rulers of this age…. Now we have received not the spirit of the world, but the Spirit who is from God, that we might understand the things freely given us by God. And we impart this in words not taught by human wisdom but taught by the Spirit, interpreting spiritual truths to those who are spiritual."*
> —1 Corinthians 2:6, 12–13 (ESV)

I. A WORD OF WISDOM DEFINED

Although a word of wisdom is one of the most needed gifts, it may be one of the most overlooked in our day. Joseph, Daniel, Esther, Nehemiah, and others from the Bible exhibited remarkable, God-sent wisdom. And the life of Jesus, of course, is a demonstration of the way of wisdom.

Do you have to be advanced in age before you can exercise a gift of wisdom? Not at all; the biblical leaders mentioned above were in the prime of their lives. Must you first attain a theological degree or achieve a certain status within the body of Christ? No, a gift of wisdom is bestowed supernaturally as the Holy Spirit determines.

Various Bible teachers (listed below in alphabetical order by their last names) have defined the gift of a word of wisdom:

A. Kenneth Hagin (late father of the Word of Faith movement)

The word of wisdom is a supernatural revelation by the Spirit of God concerning the divine *purpose* and plan in the mind and will of God. The word of wisdom is

56

the best gift because it is a revelation concerning the plans and the purposes in the mind of God.[1]

B. Dick Iverson (author, founding pastor of City Bible Church [Oregon], formerly called Portland Bible Temple)

The gift of the word of wisdom is supernaturally given by God. It is not *"a"* word of wisdom but *"the"* word of wisdom. It is not just a word on the subject or the situation at hand, it is *"the word"* on it. It is the answer, the solution, or the will of God in that situation.[2]

C. Derek Prince (late author, international Bible teacher)

We need the gift of a word of wisdom because we are supposed to be solution people, not problem people. For example, when prophets are predicting times of upheaval and desperation, we need God's wise spokespeople to help us understand what to do. The church needs to provide God's solutions, not just diagnose the problems (which the world already spends most of its time doing). Derek Prince made a useful distinction between knowledge and wisdom:

Knowledge gives us facts and wisdom shows us what to do about those facts....

...The gift of a word of wisdom...is a tiny portion of God's total wisdom directly and supernaturally imparted by the Holy Spirit.[3]

D. David Pytches (Anglican bishop, author)

The gift of the word of wisdom is the special ability that God gives to members of the body of Christ to receive instant insight on how a given revelation (word of knowledge, prophecy) may best be applied to a specific situation or need arising in the body of Christ, or how a given situation or need is to be resolved or helped or healed.[4]

E. Sam Storms (author, Bible teacher, former visiting associate professor of theology at Wheaton College)

We can appreciate Sam Storms' particular slant on the gift because it emphasizes the *giving* aspect more than the *receiving* aspect. The gift of a word of wisdom enables people to speak clearly and compellingly about God's all-wise purposes, conveying His loving guidance to whole governments (as Joseph did in Egypt) as well as to individuals within the church.

[The] word of wisdom may be the ability to articulate life-changing insights into God's mysterious, saving purposes for mankind, both on a global plane as well as in application to individuals.[5]

F.   Peter Wagner (missiologist, author, apostolic teacher)

The gift of wisdom is the special ability that God gives to certain members of the body of Christ to know the mind of the Holy Spirit in such a way as to receive insight into how given knowledge may be best applied to specific needs arising in the body of Christ (see Acts 6:3, 10; 1 Cor. 2:1–13; 12:8; James 1:5–6; 2 Pet. 3:15–16).[6]

G.   John Wimber (late author, international Vineyard leader)

"*'For My thoughts are not your thoughts, nor are your ways My ways,' declares the* LORD" (Isaiah 55:8). Wimber points out that God's wisdom is totally "transrational":

The word of wisdom is an utterance inspired by God and spoken by an individual. It reveals a part of the total wisdom of God. It reveals what God sees in a given situation. It is supernatural insight, transrational in nature.[7]

II. EXAMPLES OF A WORD OF WISDOM

A.   Scripture abounds with examples of this gift in action. Solomon exhibited supernatural wisdom in judging the case of the two women who disputed over the one living child. Justice was the result.

Then the king said, "Get me a sword." So they brought a sword before the king. The king said, "Divide the living child in two, and give half to the one and half to the other." Then the woman whose child was the living one spoke to the king, for she was deeply stirred over her son and said, "Oh, my lord, give her the living child, and by no means kill him." But the other said, "He shall be neither mine nor yours; divide him!" Then the king said, "Give the first woman the living child, and by no means kill him. She is his mother." When all Israel heard of the judgment which the king had handed down, they feared the king, for they saw that the wisdom of God was in him to administer justice.

(1 Kings 3:24–28)

B.   Jesus gave a word of wisdom that confounded His opponents. (Marveling or being confounded are common responses from those who witness the operation of this gift.)

Then the Pharisees went and plotted together how they might trap Him in what He said. And they sent their disciples to Him, along with the Herodians, saying, "Teacher, we know that You are truthful and teach the way of God in truth, and defer to no one; for You are not partial to any. Tell us then, what do You think? Is it lawful to give a poll-tax to Caesar, or not?" But Jesus perceived their malice, and said, "Why are you testing

Me, you hypocrites? Show Me the coin used for the poll-tax." And they brought Him a denarius. And He said to them, "Whose likeness and inscription is this?" They said to Him, "Caesar's." Then He said to them, "Then render to Caesar the things that are Caesar's; and to God the things that are God's." And hearing this, they were amazed, and leaving Him, they went away.   (Matthew 22:15–22)

C.   The early church relied on this gift over and over. Nobody had ever done what they were doing; there was no precedent for them to follow. So, they did the best thing they could do—they depended on the Spirit for direction.

At one point, the church leaders were being stretched too thin as the apostles had to divide their time between preaching and caring for the needy widows. Scripture does not say, "The apostles started looking for strong volunteers who had the gift of helps/service." Instead, undoubtedly guided by wisdom from on high, they advised the people to look for men who had the gift of *wisdom* who could take care of the distribution of food. They specifically wanted high-caliber men of wisdom to perform practical tasks:

*So the twelve summoned the congregation of the disciples and said, "It is not desirable for us to neglect the word of God in order to serve tables. Therefore, brethren, select from among you seven men of good reputation, **full of the Spirit and of wisdom**, whom we may put in charge of this task.*   (Acts 6:2–3)

III. HOW A WORD OF WISDOM IS RECEIVED AND RELEASED

A.   By the Spirit Speaking Within

Often, we "hear" the Spirit's voice as no more than a divine impression, perceived in our heart through spiritual intuition, like a quiet "nudge." This is the way the early apostles were led, too, as we can see in these instances:

They [Paul and those who were traveling with him] passed through the Phrygian and Galatian region, having been forbidden by the Holy Spirit to speak the word in Asia; and after they came to Mysia, they were trying to go into Bithynia, and the Spirit of Jesus did not permit them.   (Acts 16:6–7)

And now, behold, bound by the Spirit, I am on my way to Jerusalem, not knowing what will happen to me there....   (Acts 20:22)

The Spirit did not say, "Thou shalt not!" from the midst of a thundercloud. His guiding hand was not obvious, but they had learned to be as sensitive to His subtle pressures as well-trained, obedient horses are to the slight tugs and pulls of their masters' reins.

B. By a "Quickened" Word of Scripture

Sometimes, a word or line of Scripture speaks directly to our situation; it comes alive, as if God were speaking directly to us (which He is). This is called a "quickened" word from the Lord. An example of this is when Peter advised the early church about replacing Judas. He quoted a couple of psalms that applied to the situation at hand. (See Acts 1:15–26.) Later, after Peter had brought some Gentiles to the faith, which distressed the members of the church who were staunchly Jewish, James quoted the prophet Amos to defend him. Luke recorded how James rendered a wise decision based on that word of Scripture:

> *After they had stopped speaking, James answered, saying, "Brethren, listen to me. Simeon has related how God first concerned Himself about taking from among the Gentiles a people for His name. With this the words of the Prophets agree, just as it is written, 'After these things I will return, and I will rebuild the tabernacle of David which has fallen, and I will rebuild its ruins, and I will restore it, so that the rest of mankind may seek the Lord, and all the Gentiles who are called by My name,' says the Lord, who makes these things known from long ago. Therefore it is my judgment that we do not trouble those who are turning to God from among the Gentiles."*
>
> (Acts 15:13–19, quoting Amos 9:11–12)

C. By an Angel or an Audible Voice

Sometimes, God speaks through an angel, as He did when Paul was on board the storm-lashed ship that looked like it was going to sink. (See Acts 27:21–24.) Other times, He speaks directly and audibly to a person, as He did to Elijah:

> *After the earthquake a fire, but the LORD was not in the fire; and after the fire a sound of a gentle blowing. When Elijah heard it, he wrapped his face in his mantle and went out and stood in the entrance of the cave. And behold, a voice came to him and said, "What are you doing here, Elijah?" Then he said, "I have been very zealous for the LORD, the God of hosts; for the sons of Israel have forsaken Your covenant, torn down Your altars and killed Your prophets with the sword. And I alone am left; and they seek my life, to take it away." The LORD said to him, "Go, return on your way to the wilderness of Damascus, and when you have arrived, you shall anoint Hazael king over Aram; and Jehu the son of Nimshi you shall anoint king over Israel; and Elisha the son of Shaphat of Abel-meholah you shall anoint as prophet in your place. It shall come about, the one who escapes from the sword of Hazael, Jehu shall put to death, and the one who escapes from the sword of Jehu, Elisha shall put to death. Yet I will leave 7,000 in Israel, all the knees that have not bowed to Baal and every mouth that has not kissed him."* (1 Kings 19:12–18)

D. By Dreams, Visions, or Trances

God sometimes sends a word of wisdom by means of a vision or a dream (which is a vision received during sleep). This is how the Spirit reassured Paul when he was working in Corinth:

The Lord said to Paul in the night by a vision, "Do not be afraid any longer, but go on speaking and do not be silent; for I am with you, and no man will attack you in order to harm you, for I have many people in this city."   (Acts 18:9–10)

Also remember another scriptural example—the time the Spirit directed Peter to go to the home of the devout Roman centurion Cornelius through a vision that Peter received while in a trance. (See Acts 10:1–23.)

E.   By the Unanimity of the Spirit Among Spiritual Leaders

Sometimes, the gift of a word of wisdom can only be exercised corporately, as when leaders discuss and work together to arrive at a decision by consensus. They take counsel together, which is good, because *"in a multitude of counselors there is safety"* (Proverbs 24:6 NKJV; see also Proverbs 11:14 NKJV). This keeps headstrong individuals from taking off in the wrong direction and dragging other people with them. We see this method of wisdom-seeking in the accounts of the early church, as *"the apostles and the elders met together to consider this matter"* (Acts 15:6 NRSV). In fact, all of Acts chapter 15 shows corporate wisdom in action. (See also Acts 21:15–25.)

Let us now look again at the incident in which wisdom was given to the apostles concerning the needy widows, a situation that ended with unanimity in the Spirit:

Now…a complaint arose on the part of the Hellenistic Jews against the native Hebrews, because their widows were being overlooked in the daily serving of food. So the twelve summoned the congregation of the disciples and said, "It is not desirable for us to neglect the word of God in order to serve tables. Therefore, brethren, select from among you seven men of good reputation, full of the Spirit and of wisdom, whom we may put in charge of this task. But we will devote ourselves to prayer and to the ministry of the word." **The statement found approval with the whole congregation;** *and they chose Stephen, a man full of faith and of the Holy Spirit, and Philip, Prochorus, Nicanor, Timon, Parmenas and Nicolas, a proselyte from Antioch.*   (Acts 6:1–5)

IV. SUMMARY STATEMENTS

A.   Wisdom is imparted from God in order to solve the individual's, the church's, and even a nation's problems and complex situations.

B.   It is vital for believers to immerse themselves in the knowledge and wisdom of the written Word.

C.   Wisdom blends with the other gifts of the Spirit, creating endless variety.

The gifts of the Spirit are like the colors of a magnificent rainbow, blended together by the Spirit as needed to achieve the required result for any given situation. It can be difficult to determine where one gift (especially a revelational gift such as discerning of spirits, a word of wisdom, or a word of knowledge) leaves off and another picks up.

D. **Wisdom is greatly needed in times of change. It produces conviction, unanimity, progress, success, open hearts, open doors, justice, perspective, peace, and much more.**

E. **Wisdom is not the same as prediction, although without a doubt, God knows what is going to happen.**

When God sends us His wisdom for a situation, He is helping to direct our steps. He wants us to cooperate with Him for the sake of spreading His kingdom on earth; this cooperation can span every category of human involvement, from personal health decisions to international war alliances. So we see that wisdom often concerns future events and developments, but it does not foretell them as much as it supplies insights, revelations, commands, and instructions that arise out of God's knowledge of those upcoming circumstances.

F. **Jesus is *"the way, and the truth, and the life"* (John 14:6). The Spirit of this God-Man now lives in every Christian; Jesus has become to us God's wisdom:**

> *And because of him [God] you are in Christ Jesus, who became to us wisdom from God, righteousness and sanctification and redemption, so that, as it is written, "Let the one who boasts, boast in the Lord."* (1 Corinthians 1:30–31 esv)

Furthermore, *"we have the mind of Christ"*:

> *"For who has understood the mind of the Lord so as to instruct him?" But we have the mind of Christ.* (1 Corinthians 2:16 esv)

We can apply Paul's prayer for the Ephesians to ourselves and to anyone we pray for:

> *I keep asking that the God of our Lord Jesus Christ, the glorious Father, may give you the Spirit of wisdom and revelation, so that you may know him better. I pray that the eyes of your heart may be enlightened in order that you may know the hope to which he has called you, the riches of his glorious inheritance in his holy people, and his incomparably great power for us who believe.* (Ephesians 1:17–19 niv)

LESSON FIVE: THE GIFT OF A WORD OF WISDOM

(Answers to these questions can be found in the back of the study guide.)

Fill in the Blank

1. "Knowledge gives us facts and _____ shows us what to do about those facts."

2. In your own words, define the gift of a word of wisdom:

    _____

    _____

3. List three scriptural examples of the operation of a word of wisdom (see "**II. EXAMPLES OF A WORD OF WISDOM**"):

    (a) _____

    (b) _____

    (c) _____

Multiple Choice—Choose the best answer from the list below:

A—God   C—gifts

B—dreams   D—human intellect

4.   All wisdom comes from _____.

5.   True wisdom amazes and confounds _____.

True or False

6.   Solomon used the gift of discernment in judging between
the two women.   **T / F**

7.   A word of wisdom produces conviction, unanimity,
progress, open hearts, open doors, and justice.   **T / F**

8.   Words of wisdom always come through dreams.   **T/ F**

Scripture Memorization

Write out Ephesians 1:17–19 and memorize it. Use whatever version of Scripture is most familiar to you. Here is the passage in the *New International Version:*

> *I keep asking that the God of our Lord Jesus Christ, the glorious Father, may give you the Spirit of wisdom and revelation, so that you may know him better. I pray that the eyes of your heart may be enlightened in order that you may know the hope to which he has called you, the riches of his glorious inheritance in his holy people, and his incomparably great power for us who believe.*

Lesson Six

THE GIFT OF A
WORD OF KNOWLEDGE

*"My goal is that they may be encouraged in heart and united in love, so that they may have
the full riches of complete understanding, in order that they may know the mystery of God,
namely, Christ, in whom are hidden all the treasures of wisdom and knowledge."*
—Colossians 2:2–3 (NIV)

I. THE GIFT OF A WORD OF KNOWLEDGE DEFINED

No way could any human being—even the smartest person the world has ever seen—know everything. But God does. He is omniscient, knowing all things, even the deepest secrets. And through the gift of a word of knowledge, He shares parts of His knowledge with His sons and daughters.

The gift of a word of knowledge "pertains to *information*" (as compared to a word of wisdom, which "pertains to instruction" about what to do with the information).[1] This gift is often used in conjunction with healing ministry, but it has broad application within the body of Christ. Various teachers have defined the gift as follows (names listed in alphabetical order):

A. Kenneth Hagin (late father of the Word of Faith movement)

The word of knowledge is *the supernatural revelation by the Holy Ghost of certain facts in the mind of God....* A word of knowledge would simply be a fragmentary part of the entire knowledge or counsel of God.[2]

B.   Dick Iverson (author, founding pastor of City Bible Church [Oregon], formerly called Portland Bible Temple)

The word of knowledge is the supernatural revelation to man of some detail of the knowledge of God. It is the impartation of facts and information which are humanly impossible to know.... It is knowledge that surpasses the senses of man.[3]

C.   Derek Prince (late author, international Bible teacher)

A word of knowledge...is a tiny portion of God's total knowledge supernaturally imparted by the Holy Spirit....

Like a word of wisdom, supernatural knowledge does not come by natural reasoning, education, or training but directly by the Holy Spirit, and it is operated only under God's control.[4]

D.   David Pytches (Anglican bishop, author)

[The gift of a word of knowledge] is the supernatural revelation of facts about a person or situation, which is not learned through the efforts of the natural mind, but is a fragment of knowledge freely given by God, disclosing the truth which the Spirit wishes to be made known concerning a particular person or situation. (Adopted from John Wimber.)[5]

E.   Sam Storms (author, Bible teacher, former visiting associate professor of theology at Wheaton College)

The customary Pentecostal, charismatic, third-wave understanding of the word of wisdom and the word of knowledge is that they refer, respectively, to the articulation of revelatory insight in the *how* (wisdom) and *what* (knowledge) of a person's life. Word of wisdom, so it has been said, pertains to *instruction* and word of knowledge pertains to *information*.[6]

F.   Peter Wagner (missiologist, author, apostolic teacher)

The gift of knowledge is the special ability that God gives to certain members of the Body of Christ to discover, accumulate, analyze and clarify information and ideas that are pertinent to the growth and well-being of the Body (see Acts 5:1–11; 1 Cor. 2:14; 12:8; 2 Cor. 11:6; Col. 2:2–3).[7]

(In Wagner's view, this gift is used largely by "knowledge workers" in the church, such as scholars.)

G.   John Wimber (late author, international Vineyard leader)

> A word of knowledge is an utterance inspired by God and spoken by an individual. It is an insight into the things freely given us by God. It shares the truth the Spirit wishes declared concerning a specific occasion, person, or thing.[8]

The church has understood the gift of a word of knowledge in at least two distinct ways. Some focus on the gift as a supernatural facility to gather and disseminate important information for the sake of the body of Christ. Those who hold this point of view would say that the typical Pentecostal/charismatic explanation of a "word of knowledge"—namely, that it refers to a revelation of details about a person's life or a situation—should really be considered a subset of the gifts of prophecy and discernment.

This study guide follows the Pentecostal/charismatic/third-wave approach to the gift of a word of knowledge. Looking at it in this way, a word of knowledge is the gift that is used to "call out" someone for further ministry in a meeting in which the spiritual gifts are active. The revelation of details that could not otherwise be known by the speaker, such as a person's name, physical circumstances, and hidden needs, provides convincing proof that God wants to bless that person beyond his or her limited expectations.

Regardless of what kind of knowledge we mean, the fact that the word of knowledge is a spiritual gift signals the fact that this knowledge is supernaturally derived.

> *Now there are varieties of gifts, but the same Spirit; and there are varieties of service* ["ministries" NASB], *but the same Lord; and there are varieties of activities, but it is the same God who empowers them all in everyone.*   (1 Corinthians 12:4–6 ESV)

II. EXAMPLES OF THE GIFT OF A WORD OF KNOWLEDGE IN ACTION

A.   Jesus and Nathanael. Result: *Conviction*

> *Jesus saw Nathanael coming toward Him, and said of him, "Behold, an Israelite indeed, in whom is no deceit!" Nathanael said to Him, "How do You know me?" Jesus answered and said to him, "Before Philip called you, when you were under the fig tree, I saw you." Nathanael answered and said to Him, "Rabbi, You are the Son of God! You are the King of Israel!"*   (John 1:47–49 NKJV)

B.   Jesus and the Samaritan Woman at the Well. Result: *Conviction*

> *The woman said to him, "Sir, give me this water so that I won't get thirsty and have to keep coming here to draw water." He told her, "Go, call your husband and come back." "I have no husband," she replied. Jesus said to her, "You are right when you say you*

have no husband. The fact is, you have had five husbands, and the man you now have is not your husband. What you have just said is quite true." "Sir," the woman said, "I can see that you are a prophet.... I know that Messiah" (called Christ) "is coming. When he comes, he will explain everything to us." Then Jesus declared, "I, the one speaking to you—I am he." (John 4:15–19, 25–26 NIV)

C. Paul, Bound for Jerusalem. Result: *Preparation*

[Paul said,] "And now, compelled by the Spirit, I am going to Jerusalem, not knowing what will happen to me there. I only know that in every city the Holy Spirit warns me that prison and hardships are facing me." (Acts 20:22–23 NIV)

After we had been there a number of days, a prophet named Agabus came down from Judea. Coming over to us, he took Paul's belt, tied his own hands and feet with it and said, "The Holy Spirit says, 'In this way the Jewish leaders in Jerusalem will bind the owner of this belt and will hand him over to the Gentiles.'" (Acts 21:10–11 NIV)

D. Jesus and the Scribes. Result: *Revealing Knowledge About a Situation*

And at once some of the scribes said within themselves, "This Man blasphemes!" But Jesus, knowing their thoughts, said, "Why do you think evil in your hearts? For which is easier, to say, 'Your sins are forgiven you,' or to say, 'Arise and walk'?" (Matthew 9:3–5 NKJV)

III. HOW THE GIFT OF A WORD OF KNOWLEDGE IS RECEIVED AND RELEASED

A. By a Vision or a Dream

[The Lord said,] "I have also spoken by the prophets, and have multiplied visions; I have given symbols through the witness of the prophets." (Hosea 12:10 NKJV)

The words of Amos, one of the shepherds of Tekoa—the vision he saw concerning Israel two years before the earthquake, when Uzziah was king of Judah and Jeroboam son of Jehoash was king of Israel. (Amos 1:1 NIV)

The next day, as they went on their journey and drew near the city, Peter went up on the housetop to pray, about the sixth hour. Then he became very hungry and wanted to eat; but while they made ready, he fell into a trance and saw heaven opened and an object like a great sheet bound at the four corners, descending to him and let down to the earth. In it were all kinds of four-footed animals of the earth, wild beasts, creeping things, and birds of the air. And a voice came to him, "Rise, Peter; kill and eat." But Peter said, "Not so, Lord! For I have never eaten anything common or unclean." And a voice spoke to him again the second time, "What God has cleansed you must not call common." This was done three times. And the object was taken up into heaven again. Now while Peter wondered within himself what this vision which he had seen meant, behold, the men who had been sent from Cornelius had made inquiry for Simon's house, and stood before the gate. And they called and asked whether Simon, whose surname was Peter, was lodging there. While Peter thought about the vision, the Spirit said to him, "Behold, three men are seeking you. Arise therefore, go down and go with them, doubting nothing; for I have sent them."   (Acts 10:9–20 NKJV)

B.   By an Audible Voice, or by an Angel

In such cases, the delivery system is much more dramatic, and the recipient hears a word of knowledge spoken in audible words, in his or her own language.

C.   By an Impression

Most of the time, a word of knowledge comes by a quiet impression or sense. You could call this "hearing internally," or having a "gut feeling." You just "know that you know," but not how you know it. Depending on what the Holy Spirit indicates, you might share this sense with others, or you might not.

D.   By the "Quickening" of the Scriptures

Such an internal knowing as described above in "C" may well be confirmed by a "quickening" of a passage of Scripture, as happens with other kinds of senses from the Spirit. The psalmist said, *"Open my eyes, so that I may behold wondrous things out of your law"* (Psalm 119:18 NRSV). Let's review two New Testament passages that show how the apostles received a quickened word:

In those days Peter stood up among the believers (a group numbering about a hundred and twenty) and said, "Brothers and sisters, the Scripture had to be fulfilled in which the Holy Spirit spoke long ago through David concerning Judas, who served as guide for those who arrested Jesus. He was one of our number and shared in our ministry."… "For," said Peter, "it is written in the Book of Psalms: 'May his place be deserted; let there be no one to dwell in it,' and, 'May another take his place of leadership.' Therefore it is necessary to choose one of the men who have been with us the whole time the Lord Jesus was living among us, beginning from John's baptism to the time when Jesus was taken up from us. For one of these must become a witness with us of his resurrection."   (Acts 1:15–17, 20–22 NIV)

James spoke up. "Brothers," he said, "listen to me. Simon has described to us how God first intervened to choose a people for his name from the Gentiles. The words of the prophets are in agreement with this, as it is written: 'After this I will return and rebuild

David's fallen tent. Its ruins I will rebuild, and I will restore it, that the rest of mankind may seek the Lord, even all the Gentiles who bear my name, says the Lord, who does these things'—things known from long ago. It is my judgment, therefore, that we should not make it difficult for the Gentiles who are turning to God." (Acts 15:13–19 NIV)

E. By Empathetic "Sensings"—Feelings in One's Physical Body

Sometimes, especially if a word of knowledge has to do with healing, you might receive empathetic "signals" in your own body—physical or emotional—such as a noticeable pain that you didn't have before or an oppressive feeling. This physical sense can indicate God's intention toward a specific individual or a group of people.

F. By the "Spirit of Counsel"

One of the most common expressions of this gift is what I would call the "spirit of counsel." A deposit of a word of knowledge is given when someone is writing a letter, counseling, or praying for or about someone else. The word is first received and then shared at the instigation of the Holy Spirit, and it provides godly help for the recipient. In such cases, you can see how closely it becomes allied with the gift of a word of wisdom.

IV. INSTRUCTIONS FOR OPERATING IN THE GIFT OF A WORD OF KNOWLEDGE

A. Timing Is Essential

The fact that something has been revealed to you does not necessarily mean it should be spoken immediately, or even at all. Always seek the Lord for confirmation about the timing of the release of any word of knowledge.

B. Wisdom Complements the Application

A word of knowledge is not necessarily complete in itself. Therefore (as was shared in the previous lesson) wisdom should be sought as to what to do, where to share it, and more. Sometimes, outside advice should be sought, as when the word of knowledge will have an impact on a decision that will affect the lives of other people.

C. Submit Words of Knowledge for Discernment

Particularly in church governmental or corrective issues, a word of knowledge should be submitted to the proper authorities for them to confirm the word and determine the appropriate application. It is all-important to respect the other members of the body around you. We need to walk with each other and to build a history together. Mutual trust is earned over time.

D. Avoid Self-Exaltation

Receiving knowledge directly from God can be a heady experience, but it does not put a person into an elite category. In the body of Christ, no one person should be a star. No one person should talk too much. Excessive verbiage almost always stems from insecurity. Everyone should make it a priority to find personal security in God's love, rather than in human adulation.

E. Be Tenacious

Even in the name of avoiding self-exaltation, no one should be afraid to speak out a word of knowledge. We need to step out in faith; it's the only way to learn the ropes. We need to be flat-out tenacious about growing in our gifts. *"Make every effort,"* as Peter said:

> *Make every effort to add to your faith goodness; and to goodness, knowledge; and to knowledge, self-control; and to self-control, perseverance; and to perseverance, godliness; and to godliness, mutual affection; and to mutual affection, love. For if you possess these qualities in increasing measure, they will keep you from being ineffective and unproductive in your knowledge of our Lord Jesus Christ. But whoever does not have them is nearsighted and blind, forgetting that they have been cleansed from their past sins. Therefore, my brothers and sisters, make every effort to confirm your calling and election. For if you do these things, you will never stumble, and you will receive a rich welcome into the eternal kingdom of our Lord and Savior Jesus Christ.*
>
> (2 Peter 1:5–11 NIV)

Using our gifts is part of growing in holiness, and growing in holiness enhances our use of God's gifts. We should learn from our mistakes and mature in all things having to do with Christ Jesus.

Even if a word of knowledge never gets delivered, it can inform intercessory prayer. As always, humility matters. Believers' spheres of influence and their effectiveness will never be identical. You may never have the honor of speaking out a word of knowledge or prophecy, but that is not the kind of honor you should desire, anyway. *Honor lies in God trusting you.*

We can regularly expect words of knowledge to weave through our daily lives. How gracious of the Spirit to give them to us. May we learn to spot them so we can use them appropriately—and so we can thank the Giver of the gift.

Questions for Reflection

LESSON SIX: THE GIFT OF A WORD OF KNOWLEDGE

(Answers to these questions can be found in the back of the study guide.)

Fill in the Blank

1. *"For to one is given the word of wisdom through the Spirit, and to another the _____ __ _____ according to the same Spirit"* (1 Corinthians 12:8).

2. Write your own definition of the gift of a word of knowledge:

   _____

   _____

   _____

3. List three purposes (results) of the gift of a word of knowledge:

   (a) _____

   (b) _____

   (c) _____

Multiple Choice—Choose the best answer from the list below:

A—mantle   C—counsel

B—utterance   D—revelation

4.   A word of knowledge is a supernatural _____ of certain facts.

5.   One of the most common expressions of the gift is the "spirit of _____."

True or False

6.   A word of knowledge is complete in itself and does
     not require supplementation or corroboration.   **T / F**

7.   A word of knowledge should always be spoken.   **T / F**

8.   In church governmental or corrective issues,
     a word of knowledge should be submitted to
     the proper authorities.   **T / F**

Scripture Memorization

Write out Colossians 2:2–3 and memorize it. You may prefer to memorize a different Scripture translation. This passage is in the *New International Version*.

My goal is that they may be encouraged in heart and united in love, so that they may have the full riches of complete understanding, in order that they may know the mystery of God, namely, Christ, in whom are hidden all the treasures of wisdom and knowledge.

POWER GIFTS—THE GIFTS THAT DO

"Jesus said to them, 'Truly, truly, I say to you, the Son can do nothing of his own accord, but only what he sees the Father doing. For whatever the Father does, that the Son does likewise.'"
—John 5:19 (ESV)

The hardworking spiritual gifts of faith, healings, and workings of miracles are active when believers (1) stir themselves to listen to the Holy Spirit to find out what the Father is doing, and (2) obey the direction He gives them. This is why we see so much variety in the outworking of these gifts. Believers do not follow prescribed rules and guidelines—they follow God. The sky (or more!) is the limit, and all the credit goes to Him.

This is why Paul wrote, *"I will not presume to speak of anything except what Christ has accomplished through me...in the power of signs and wonders, in the power of the Spirit"* (Romans 15:18–19).

THE GIFT OF FAITH

"Then the disciples came to Jesus in private and asked, 'Why couldn't we drive it out?'
He replied, 'Because you have so little faith. Truly I tell you, if you have faith as small as a
mustard seed, you can say to this mountain, "Move from here to there," and it will move.
Nothing will be impossible for you.'"
—Matthew 17:19–20 (NIV)

I. THE GIFT OF FAITH DEFINED

It can sometimes be difficult to differentiate the spiritual gift of faith from the measure of faith that is common to every believer (without which we could not even come to a saving faith). Various Bible teachers (listed below in alphabetical order) explain what to look for in the gift of faith:

A. Kenneth Hagin (late father of the Word of Faith movement)

[The gift of faith] is a supernatural manifestation of the Holy Spirit whereby a believer is empowered with *special* faith…. The gift of faith is a gift of the Spirit to the believer in order that he might *receive* miracles…. Those who operate in special faith…can believe God in such a way that *God* honors their word as His own, and miraculously brings to pass the desired result.[1]

B. Dick Iverson (author, founding pastor of City Bible Church [Oregon], formerly called Portland Bible Temple)

The gift of faith is the God-given ability to believe Him for the impossible in a particular situation. It is not so much the general faith which believes God for provision, but goes a step beyond, where one *just knows* that a particular thing is the will of God and is going to happen.[2]

C. Derek Prince (late author, international Bible teacher)

God has all faith, and through this gift He imparts to us a tiny portion of it.... This is faith that comes instantly, supernaturally, as a gift directly from God by the Holy Spirit, very frequently in the form of a word. This gift...is operated only under God's control.[3]

Derek Prince also explained that the gift of faith is different from the faith essential for salvation or the faith that is a fruit of the Holy Spirit. It is a miraculous, "mountain-moving gift."[4]

D. David Pytches (Anglican bishop, author)

This gift is a supernatural surge of confidence from the Spirit of God which arises within a person faced with a specific situation or need, whereby that person receives a transrational certainty and assurance that God is about to act through a word or action. This miracle utterance covers creation or destruction, blessing or cursing, removal or alteration.[5]

E. Sam Storms (author, Bible teacher, former visiting associate professor of theology at Wheaton College)

Charismatic faith is the faith...that appears to be spontaneous and functions as the divinely enabled condition on which the more overtly supernatural activities of God are suspended....

The gift of faith is that mysterious surge of confidence that rises within a person in a particular situation of need or challenge and which gives an extraordinary certainty and assurance that God is about to act through a word or an action.[6]

F. Peter Wagner (missiologist, author, apostolic teacher)

The gift of faith is the special ability that God gives certain members of the Body of Christ to discern with extraordinary confidence the will and purposes of God for the future of His work (see Acts 11:22–24; 27:21–25; Rom. 4:18–21; 1 Cor. 12:9; Heb. 11).[7]

G. John Wimber (late author, international Vineyard leader)

The gift of faith is the mysterious surge of confidence which sometimes arises within a person faced with a specific situation or need. It gives that person a transrational (otherly) certainty and assurance that God is about to act through a word of action. It is both the irresistible knowledge that God wills to intervene at a certain point and the authority to effect this intervention through the power of the Holy Spirit.[8]

II. CATEGORIES OF FAITH

Consider these various categories of faith:

A. The Measure of Faith That Each Believer Receives

> *I say, through the grace given to me, to everyone who is among you, not to think of himself more highly than he ought to think, but to think soberly, as God has dealt to each one a measure of faith.*   (Romans 12:3 NKJV; see also Romans 14:1–2)

When our measure of faith is exercised faithfully, it grows, and it bears abundant fruit. It may start out very small, but it can accomplish great things. Jesus said,

> *Truly I tell you, if you have faith as small as a mustard seed, you can say to this mountain, "Move from here to there," and it will move. Nothing will be impossible for you.*
> (Matthew 17:20 NIV)

The goal is maturity of faith:

> *…till we all come to the unity of the faith and of the knowledge of the Son of God, to a perfect man, to the measure of the stature of the fullness of Christ.*   (Ephesians 4:13 NKJV)

B. The Fruit of Faithfulness—Grown over Time

If you are truly "faith-full," you will be filled with two kinds of faith: faith in God's ability to do amazing things, and also faithfulness (i.e., dependability). The latter kind of faith is a character trait, an attribute of a person of covenant loyalty, whose word is bond. *"The fruit of the Spirit is…faithfulness"* (Galatians 5:22).

> *And I will betroth you to Me in faithfulness. Then you will know the LORD.*
> (Hosea 2:20)

> *Righteousness will be his belt and faithfulness the sash around his waist.*
> (Isaiah 11:5 NIV)

> *Let love and faithfulness never leave you; bind them around your neck, write them on the tablet of your heart.*   (Proverbs 3:3 NIV)

C. The Gift of Faith—Imparted According to Need and Function

This gift of faith, this supernatural confidence-surge, makes it possible for a person to pray or declare God's will and to thereby effect miraculous blessings—or cursing and destruction.[9]

We would prefer to think only of the blessings and creative miracles, but remember that faith power can also toss mountains into the sea or wither fig trees within hours:

> *And Jesus answered saying to them, "Have faith in God. Truly I say to you, whoever says to this mountain, 'Be taken up and cast into the sea,' and does not doubt in his heart, but believes that what he says is going to happen, it will be granted him."*
>
> (Mark 11:22–23)

> *Seeing in the distance a fig tree in leaf, [Jesus] went to see whether perhaps he would find anything on it. When he came to it, he found nothing but leaves, for it was not the season for figs. He said to it, "May no one ever eat fruit from you again." And his disciples heard it…. In the morning as they passed by, they saw the fig tree withered away to its roots. Then Peter remembered and said to him, "Rabbi, look! The fig tree that you cursed has withered." Jesus answered them, "Have faith in God."*
>
> (Mark 11:13–14, 20–22 NRSV)

When God plants a word of faith in a person's heart, and the person utters it aloud, the word will manifest itself in results:

> *For I am the Lord; I will speak the word that I will speak, and it will be performed. It will no longer be delayed, but in your days, O rebellious house, I will speak the word and perform it, declares the Lord God.* (Ezekiel 12:25 ESV)

III. EXAMPLES OF THE GIFT OF FAITH

A. Jesus Raising Lazarus from the Dead

> *[Jesus] said to them, "Our friend Lazarus has fallen asleep, but I go to awaken him." The disciples said to him, "Lord, if he has fallen asleep, he will recover." Now Jesus had spoken of his death, but they thought that he meant taking rest in sleep. Then Jesus told them plainly, "Lazarus has died, and for your sake I am glad that I was not there, so that you may believe. But let us go to him."… And he said, "Where have you laid him?" They said to him, "Lord, come and see." Jesus wept. So the Jews said, "See how he loved him!" But some of them said, "Could not he who opened the eyes of the blind man also have kept this man from dying?"… So they took away the stone. And Jesus lifted up his eyes and said, "Father, I thank you that you have heard me. I knew that you always hear me, but I said this on account of the people standing around, that they may believe that you sent me." When he had said these things, he cried out with a loud voice, "Lazarus, come out." The man who had died came out, his hands and feet bound with linen strips, and his face wrapped with a cloth. Jesus said to them, "Unbind him, and let him go."*
>
> (John 11:11–15, 34–37, 41–44 ESV)

B. Peter Healing the Lame Man in Jesus' Name

As soon as Peter saw the lame beggar, he knew that the man would be healed. He proclaimed his healing with unflinching and unwavering faith, and then took him by the hand to lift him to his feet. Peter's faith brought about a miracle. This man, who had never before stood up on his own feet, found himself not only standing but also walking and leaping with joy:

> *Now Peter and John were going up to the temple at the ninth hour, the hour of prayer. And a man who had been lame from his mother's womb was being carried along, whom they used to set down every day at the gate of the temple which is called Beautiful, in order to beg alms of those who were entering the temple. When he saw Peter and John about to go into the temple, he began asking to receive alms. But Peter, along with John, fixed his gaze on him and said, "Look at us!" And he began to give them his attention, expecting to receive something from them. But Peter said, "I do not possess silver and gold, but what I do have I give to you: In the name of Jesus Christ the Nazarene— walk!" And seizing him by the right hand, he raised him up; and immediately his feet and his ankles were strengthened. With a leap he stood upright and began to walk; and he entered the temple with them, walking and leaping and praising God. And all the people saw him walking and praising God; and they were taking note of him as being the one who used to sit at the Beautiful Gate of the temple to beg alms, and they were filled with wonder and amazement at what had happened to him.* (Acts 3:1–10)

IV. PRACTICAL POINTS ABOUT THE GIFT OF FAITH

A. Two Ways of Exercising the Gift of Faith

It might seem to be arrogant on the part of the speaker to utter such commands as we will see below; but, by contrast, if God is behind the words through the gift of faith, the speaker is humbled by them. The speaker knows full well that his or her words alone have no power at all and in fact may sound rather foolish if God doesn't back them up with results.

1. Words spoken to God on behalf of a person, an object, or a situation.

    Out of a gift of faith, Elijah declared, in God's name, that no rain would fall in Israel, and then, after a long time of severe drought, he announced the return of the rain. He was confident in his faith, despite the seeming lack of evidence, and he persisted until the word was fulfilled entirely.

    > *Now Elijah the Tishbite, from Tishbe in Gilead, said to Ahab, "As the LORD, the God of Israel, lives, whom I serve, there will be neither dew nor rain in the next few years except at my word."… After a long time, in the third year, the word of the LORD came to Elijah: "Go and present yourself to Ahab, and I will send rain on the land."… And Elijah said to Ahab, "Go, eat and drink, for there is the sound of a heavy rain." So Ahab went off to eat and drink, but*

Elijah climbed to the top of Carmel, bent down to the ground and put his face between his knees. "Go and look toward the sea," he told his servant. And he went up and looked. "There is nothing there," he said. Seven times Elijah said, "Go back." The seventh time the servant reported, "A cloud as small as a man's hand is rising from the sea." So Elijah said, "Go and tell Ahab, 'Hitch up your chariot and go down before the rain stops you.'" Meanwhile, the sky grew black with clouds, the wind rose, a heavy rain started falling and Ahab rode off to Jezreel.   (1 Kings 17:1; 18:1, 41–45 NIV)

Elijah was a human being, even as we are. He prayed earnestly that it would not rain, and it did not rain on the land for three and a half years. Again he prayed, and the heavens gave rain, and the earth produced its crops.
(James 5:17–18 NIV)

2.   Words spoken to a person, an object, or a situation on behalf of God.

(a)   Joshua spoke to the sun and the moon on behalf of God:

On the day the LORD gave the Amorites over to Israel, Joshua said to the LORD in the presence of Israel: "Sun, stand still over Gibeon, and you, moon, over the Valley of Aijalon." So the sun stood still, and the moon stopped, till the nation avenged itself on its enemies, as it is written in the Book of Jashar. The sun stopped in the middle of the sky and delayed going down about a full day. There has never been a day like it before or since, a day when the LORD listened to a human being. Surely the LORD was fighting for Israel!
(Joshua 10:12–14 NIV)

(b)   Jesus spoke to the wind and the waves to calm a fierce storm:

And [Jesus' disciples] came to Him and awoke Him, saying, "Master, Master, we are perishing!" Then He arose and rebuked the wind and the raging of the water. And they ceased, and there was a calm. (Luke 8:24 NKJV)

B. Two General Levels, or Functions, of the Gift of Faith

1.   The faith to function in individual gifts and ministries, such as teaching, giving, prophecy, or service. (See Romans 12:6–8 under "D," below.)

2.   The faith for specific miracles or for acts that God wants to perform in given circumstances. The Bible is filled with examples of this kind of faith.

C. The Gift of Faith Leaves No Room for Doubt

And Jesus answered saying to them, "Have faith in God. Truly I say to you, whoever says to this mountain, 'Be taken up and cast into the sea,' and does not doubt in his

> *heart, but believes that what he says is going to happen, it will be granted him. Therefore I say to you, all things for which you pray and ask, believe that you have received them, and they will be granted you."* (Mark 11:22–24)

D. The Gift of Faith Does Not Operate Alone

The gift of faith operates in conjunction with other gifts. For example, it is an important adjunct to the gifts of a word of knowledge, miracles, and healings. These gifts complement one another; they never compete with each other.

> *Since we have gifts that differ according to the grace given to us, each of us is to exercise them accordingly: if prophecy, according to the proportion of his faith; if service, in his serving; or he who teaches, in his teaching; or he who exhorts, in his exhortation; he who gives, with liberality; he who leads, with diligence; he who shows mercy, with cheerfulness.* (Romans 12:6–8)

E. The Gift of Faith Operates in Many Realms

Even a person with the gift of faith does not necessarily possess the same level of faith for every circumstance. As with the other spiritual gifts, the gift of faith seems to "specialize." One person's sphere of influence might be faith for finances or faith for miracles. Another person's faith emphasis could be faith for crisis intervention through intercession. I have seen people with gifts of faith that are specific to severe weather patterns, healing, evangelism, and deliverance from evil spirits, and none of those people would find their gift operational outside of their sphere of influence. At times, the operation of the gift appears to be determined according to the presenting need or to a person's function within the body of Christ. When this happens, the gift of faith operates independently of someone's identity as a gifted person; it is faith for special miracles or for acts that God wants to perform in given circumstances. There are no limits to what this gift of faith can address and the fruit that can be borne.

V. MORE DESIRABLE THAN GOLD

When God reveals certain facts concerning His will in a circumstance, and a person "just knows" it will happen, that is the gift of faith. It is to be much sought after. Such faith is irresistible. When such knowledge is declared orally, the words do not return void. (See Isaiah 55:11 NKJV, KJV.) "They are more desirable than gold":

> *The commandment of the LORD is pure, enlightening the eyes. The fear of the LORD is clean, enduring forever; the judgments of the LORD are true; they are righteous altogether. They are more desirable than gold, yes, than much fine gold; sweeter also than honey and the drippings of the honeycomb.* (Psalm 19:8–10)

God gives the gift of faith generously, and He wants believers to recognize it when they experience it, so they will appreciate it and use it well and wisely. We should all make a point to use the measure of faith with which we have been supplied, rejoicing greatly should our circumstances or our sphere of influence require more.

LESSON SEVEN: THE GIFT OF FAITH

(Answers to these questions can be found in the back of the study guide.)

Fill in the Blank

1. In your own words, define the gift of faith:

   _____

   _____

2. *"Jesus answered saying to them, 'Have _____ in God. Truly, I say to you, whoever says to this _____, "Be taken up and cast into the sea," and does not _____ in his heart, but _____ that what he says is going to happen, it shall be _____ him'"* (Mark 11:22–23).

3. When God _____ a word of faith in a person's heart, and the person _____ ___ _____, the word will manifest itself in results.

Multiple Choice—Choose the best answer from the list below:

A—conjunction   C—confidence

B—miracles   D—trust

4. A gift of faith is a supernatural "surge of _____."

83

5.   The gift of faith operates in _____ with other gifts. For example, it is an important adjunct to the gifts of a word of knowledge, miracles, and healings.

True or False

6.   The gift of faith works the same for every believer.   **T / F**

7.   The gift of faith and saving faith are the same.   **T / F**

8.   When Joshua spoke to the sun so that it stopped moving (see Joshua 10:12–14), this occurrence could be called a result of his gift of faith.   **T / F**

Scripture Memorization

Write out Luke 17:5–6 and memorize it. This passage is from the *English Standard Version*; choose a different Scripture translation if you prefer:

The apostles said to the Lord, "Increase our faith!" And the Lord said, "If you had faith like a grain of mustard seed, you could say to this mulberry tree, 'Be uprooted and planted in the sea,' and it would obey you."

Lesson Eight

THE GIFTS OF HEALINGS

"As Peter traveled about the country, he went to visit the Lord's people who lived in Lydda. There he found a man named Aeneas, who was paralyzed and had been bedridden for eight years. 'Aeneas,' Peter said to him, 'Jesus Christ heals you. Get up and roll up your mat.' Immediately Aeneas got up. All those who lived in Lydda and Sharon saw him and turned to the Lord."
—Acts 9:32–35 (NIV)

I. THE GIFTS OF HEALINGS DEFINED

Here is a collection of definitions of gifts of healings from various Bible teachers (listed below in alphabetical order):

A. Kenneth Hagin (late father of the Word of Faith movement)

The gifts of healing are manifested for the supernatural healing of sickness and disease without any natural source or means.… The gifts of healings have nothing to do with medical science or human learning.… The healing that is supernatural doesn't come by diagnosis or by prescribing treatment. Divine healing comes by laying on of hands, anointing with oil, or sometimes just by speaking the Word.… The purpose of these gifts is to deliver the sick and to destroy the works of the devil in the human body.[1]

B. Dick Iverson (author, founding pastor of City Bible Church [Oregon], formerly called Portland Bible Temple)

The gift of healing is the God-given ability to impart healing to the physical body at specific times. It is accompanied by a measure of the gift of faith, and often, the gift of knowledge. It involves the impartation of that faith to the one who needs healing, lifting him out of the realm of doubt and unbelief, and taking appropriate steps toward healing. It is a *"manifestation of the Spirit"* (1 Corinthians 12:7) through a person and not just his own powers of persuasion.[2]

C. Derek Prince (late author, international Bible teacher)

A healing relieves the body of disease or injury. It is often imperceptible to the senses. It may also be gradual.

…Both *gifts* and *healings* are in the plural. I interpret this to mean each time a healing comes, it is a gift given through the person by whom the gift is manifested.

As with other gifts of the Spirit, gifts of healings are operated only under God's control.[3]

D. David Pytches (Anglican bishop, author)

[The gifts of healings] are channeled through human agents for the supernatural healing of diseases and infirmities to the glory of God.… Fundamental to the gifts of healings is the principle upon which Jesus operated: "The Son can do nothing by himself; he can only do what he sees his Father doing" (John 5:19).[4]

E. Sam Storms (author, Bible teacher, former visiting associate professor of theology at Wheaton College)

I believe that there is a close connection between gifts of healings (as well as the gift of miracles) and the gift of faith, which immediately precedes them in Paul's list of the charismata.…

…Evidently, Paul did not envision that a person would be endowed with one healing gift operative at all times for all diseases. His language suggests either many different gifts or powers of healing, each appropriate to and effective for its related illness, or each occurrence of healing constituting a distinct gift in its own right.[5]

F. Peter Wagner (missiologist, author, apostolic teacher)

The gift of healing is the special ability that God gives to certain members of the Body of Christ to serve as human intermediaries through whom it pleases God to cure illness and restore health apart from the use of natural means (see Acts 3:1–10; 5:12–16; 9:32–35; 28:7–10; 1 Corinthians 12:9, 28).[6]

G. John Wimber (late author, international Vineyard leader)

The gifts of healings are used to speed up the process of healing of a sick person. As there are many kinds of illnesses, so there are different healing gifts. Healing is that event or progression which a person receives in the emotional, spiritual, or physical areas of life.[7]

II. EXAMPLES OF GIFTS OF HEALINGS

A. Jesus Healing at the Pool of Bethesda:

Often enough, the person who needs healing does not even seek it out at all, or requires some gentle persuasion to accept the idea. Recall the lame man at the pool of Bethesda:

> *After these things there was a feast of the Jews, and Jesus went up to Jerusalem. Now there is in Jerusalem by the sheep gate a pool, which is called in Hebrew Bethesda, having five porticoes. In these lay a multitude of those who were sick, blind, lame, and withered, [waiting for the moving of the waters; for an angel of the Lord went down at certain seasons into the pool and stirred up the water; whoever then first, after the stirring up of the water, stepped in was made well from whatever disease with which he was afflicted.] A man was there who had been ill for thirty-eight years. When Jesus saw him lying there, and knew that he had already been a long time in that condition, He said to him, "Do you wish to get well?" The sick man answered Him, "Sir, I have no man to put me into the pool when the water is stirred up, but while I am coming, another steps down before me." Jesus said to him, "Get up, pick up your pallet and walk." Immediately the man became well, and picked up his pallet and began to walk.* (John 5:1–9)

B. Jesus Laying Hands on Everyone and Healing Them

> *At sunset, the people brought to Jesus all who had various kinds of sickness, and laying his hands on each one, he healed them.* (Luke 4:40 NIV)

Jesus is still healing people in this manner today, through gifted believers. He *"is the same yesterday, today, and forever"* (Hebrews 13:8 NKJV).

C. Paul Healing the Father of Publius

> *And it happened that the father of Publius was lying in bed afflicted with recurrent fever and dysentery; and Paul went in to see him and after he had prayed, he laid his hands on him and healed him. After this had happened, the rest of the people on the island who had diseases were coming to him and getting cured.* (Acts 28:8–9)

III. HEALING DELIVERY SYSTEMS

A.   Laying on of Hands and Prayer by Believers

The gifts of the Spirit are not limited to only some believers. It's the prerogative of all believers to have faith in God's Word and pray for the sick.

> *These signs will accompany those who have believed:…they will lay hands on the sick, and they will recover.* (Mark 16:17–18)

B.   Calling for the Elders and Anointing with Oil

Sometimes, the laying on of hands includes anointing with oil, and often the anointing is done by a church leader. Here is the scriptural precedent for that:

> *Is anyone among you sick? Then he must call for the elders of the church and they are to pray over him, anointing him with oil in the name of the Lord; and the prayer offered in faith will restore the one who is sick, and the Lord will raise him up, and if he has committed sins, they will be forgiven him.* (James 5:14–15)

> *And they [the twelve disciples] were casting out many demons and were anointing with oil many sick people and healing them.* (Mark 6:13)

B.   Receiving Communion (the Lord's Supper)

Besides direct prayer and the laying on of hands, there is basic healing power in taking the Lord's Supper. God has bound our physical well-being to our spiritual relationship with this "flesh and blood" aspect of His Son. We need to seek Him out, to desire His presence, to obey Him. One way we can obey Him is to take Communion frequently. Jesus said, *"Do this, as often as you drink it, in remembrance of Me"* (1 Corinthians 11:25). He didn't say, "As seldom as you drink it," or "Once in a while." Paul wrote *"as often as you drink it"* in the context of these familiar words:

> *For I received from the Lord that which I also delivered to you, that the Lord Jesus in the night in which He was betrayed took bread; and when He had given thanks, He broke it and said, "This is My body, which is for you; do this in remembrance of Me." In the same way He took the cup also after supper, saying, "This cup is the new covenant in My blood; do this, as often as you drink it, in remembrance of Me."*
> (1 Corinthians 11:23–25)

The health of our relationship with God and others helps to determine the health of our physical bodies:

> *Examine yourselves, and only then eat of the bread and drink of the cup. For all who eat and drink without discerning the body, eat and drink judgment against themselves.*

For this reason many of you are weak and ill, and some have died.

(1 Corinthians 11:28–30 NRSV)

Partaking of the Lord's Supper proclaims what the Lord has done through His death and resurrection. Believers receive the cleansing of forgiveness, and they forgive others. They rejoice in the fact that Jesus' blood has triumphed over the power of the Evil One. They receive and give mercy, proclaim life over themselves, and resubmit themselves to the lordship of Jesus. All of this is highly health-promoting. Healing through taking Communion? Yes, the Lord's Supper is the "meal that heals."

D. Speaking the Word

The greatest faith, according to Jesus, roots solely in the Word of God. Three types of approaches to Jesus for healing centered on the word of healing:

1.   Those who came for personal healing.

2.   Those who brought someone else for healing.

3.   Those who came for someone else but sought only the word of Jesus stating that they would be healed.

Jesus was able to speak a word of healing at a distance that was just as effective as if He had touched the sick person. When the son of a royal official was near death, the official begged Jesus to come:

The royal official said, "Sir, come down before my child dies." "Go," Jesus replied, "your son will live." The man took Jesus at his word and departed. While he was still on the way, his servants met him with the news that his boy was living. When he inquired as to the time when his son got better, they said to him, "Yesterday, at one in the afternoon, the fever left him."

(John 4:49–52 NIV)

Remember also the story of the centurion's slave, which shows us the raw power of a word of healing:

When Jesus had finished saying all this to the people who were listening, he entered Capernaum. There a centurion's servant, whom his master valued highly, was sick and about to die. The centurion heard of Jesus and sent some elders of the Jews to him, asking him to come and heal his servant. When they came to Jesus, they pleaded earnestly with him, "This man deserves to have you do this, because he loves our nation and has built our synagogue." So Jesus went with them. He was not far from the house when the centurion sent friends to say to him: "Lord, don't trouble yourself, for I do not deserve to have you come under my roof. That is why I did not even consider myself worthy to come to you. But say the word, and my servant will be healed. For I myself am a man under authority, with soldiers under me. I tell this one, 'Go,' and he goes; and that one, 'Come,' and he comes. I say to my servant, 'Do this,' and he does it." When Jesus heard this, he was amazed at him, and turning to the crowd following him, he said, "I tell you, I have not found such great faith even in Israel." Then the men who had been sent returned to the house and found the servant well. (Luke 7:1–10 NIV)

E. Special Means, such as Jesus' Garment, Peter's Shadow, and Paul's Handkerchiefs and Aprons

Occasionally (although this delivery method of healing has been abused), something other than hands can be laid on the sick, such as an item of clothing from an anointed person or even the shadow of someone who has a healing gift. These form a point of contact for the one in need. The following account took place after Jesus had been teaching publicly and performing miracles for a while, and His reputation had begun to precede Him:

> *When they got out of the boat, immediately the people recognized Him, and ran about that whole country and began to carry here and there on their pallets those who were sick, to the place they heard He was. Wherever He entered villages, or cities, or country-side, they were laying the sick in the market places, and imploring Him that they might just touch the fringe of His cloak; and as many as touched it were being cured.*
> (Mark 6:54–56)

Later, a similar thing happened with Peter and the other apostles:

> *At the hands of the apostles many signs and wonders were taking place among the people; and they were all with one accord in Solomon's portico…. [People] even carried the sick out into the streets and laid them on cots and pallets, so that when Peter came by at least his shadow might fall on any one of them. Also the people from the cities in the vicinity of Jerusalem were coming together, bringing people who were sick or afflicted with unclean spirits, and they were all being healed.* (Acts 5:12, 15–16)

In Ephesus, Paul performed "*extraordinary miracles,*" some of which were *extra*-extraordinary because they occurred by means of items of his clothing, without Paul being present. (These miracles must have happened in this way either due to direct revelation about them or because there was no other way for Paul to lay his hands on all of the sick people in the region.)

> *God was performing extraordinary miracles by the hands of Paul, so that handkerchiefs or aprons were even carried from his body to the sick, and the diseases left them and the evil spirits went out.* (Acts 19:11–12)

(Paul's handkerchief was not a cravat or a bandanna, and his "apron" was not a contemporary ladies' kitchen apron—this probably meant his tentmaker's sweat rags and his protective craftsman's apron.)

IV. LEVELS OF OPERATION OF GIFTS OF HEALINGS

Some healings are instantaneous, while others take a considerable length of time. Here are some scriptural examples of both instantaneous and gradual healing:

A. Instantaneous Healing

Then Jesus put out His hand and touched him, saying, "I am willing; be cleansed." Immediately his leprosy was cleansed. (Matthew 8:3 NKJV)

Now as soon as they had come out of the synagogue, they entered the house of Simon and Andrew, with James and John. But Simon's wife's mother lay sick with a fever, and they told Him about her at once. So He came and took her by the hand and lifted her up, and immediately the fever left her. And she served them. (Mark 1:29–31 NKJV)

The royal official said, "Sir, come down before my child dies." "Go," Jesus replied, "your son will live." The man took Jesus at his word and departed. While he was still on the way, his servants met him with the news that his boy was living. When he inquired as to the time when his son got better, they said to him, "Yesterday, at one in the afternoon, the fever left him." (John 4:49–52 NIV)

B. Gradual Healing

When Jesus prayed for a blind man, his sight returned only after a second effort:

They came to Bethsaida. Some people brought a blind man to him and begged him to touch him. He took the blind man by the hand and led him out of the village; and when he had put saliva on his eyes and laid his hands on him, he asked him, "Can you see anything?" And the man looked up and said, "I can see people, but they look like trees, walking." Then Jesus laid his hands on his eyes again; and he looked intently and his sight was restored, and he saw everything clearly. (Mark 8:22–25 NRSV)

Where healing is concerned, we need to be sure to align ourselves with God's timing. Remember how Jesus delayed before He went to raise Lazarus from the dead. (See John 11.) Evidently, it would not have been good enough to heal Lazarus' life-threatening sickness. Instead, He waited until it was "too late" so that He could perform a much more spectacular kind of healing—a resurrection.

The members of the body of Christ learn to use their gifts of healings first from the teaching and example of the New Testament, and second from accumulated experience, both vicarious and firsthand. Rather than focus on the overwhelming needs for healings that clamor for our attention, we should turn toward the Healer, the Great Physician, in order to build faith for healings.

Obviously, the gifts of healings are not meant only for church gatherings; in fact, most healings take place outside of church settings. It is so wonderfully worthwhile to learn how to use gifts of healings in everyday life.

Believers should never hesitate to call forth gifts of healings for every form of sickness they know of and also for conditions they have not heard of—all for the glory of God!

LESSON EIGHT: THE GIFTS OF HEALINGS

(Answers to these questions can be found in the back of the study guide.)

Fill in the Blank

1. In your own words, define gifts of healings:

    _____

    _____

    _____

2. List three distinct ways that healing can be imparted (at least five can be found in the lesson):

    (a) _____

    (b) _____

    (c) _____

3. What three types of approaches did people take when they came to Jesus for healing?

    (a) _____

    (b) _____

    (c) _____

Multiple Choice—Choose the best answer from the list below:

A—cleansing   C—correction

B—miracles   D—healings

4.   *"But the manifestation of the Spirit is given to each one for the profit of all:…to another faith*

     by the same Spirit, to another gifts of _____ *by the same Spirit"* (1 Corinthians 12:7,
     9 NKJV).

5.   In partaking of the Lord's Supper, believers receive the _____ of forgive-
     ness, and they forgive others. They rejoice in the fact that Jesus' blood has triumphed
     over the power of the Evil One. They receive and give mercy, proclaim life over them-
     selves, and resubmit themselves to the lordship of Jesus. All of this is highly health-pro-
     moting.

True or False

6.   Not all healing is physical. Some healing is emotional or spiritual.   **T / F**

7.   People always need to approach God directly for their own healing.   **T / F**

8.   All healing that comes from faith-filled prayer is instantaneous.   **T / F**

Scripture Memorization

Write out James 5:14–16 and memorize it. The following is from the *New King James Version*; choose a different version of Scripture if you prefer:

> *Is anyone among you sick? Let him call for the elders of the church, and let them pray
> over him, anointing him with oil in the name of the Lord. And the prayer of faith will
> save the sick, and the Lord will raise him up. And if he has committed sins, he will be
> forgiven. Confess your trespasses to one another, and pray for one another, that you may
> be healed. The effective, fervent prayer of a righteous man avails much.*

THE WORKINGS OF MIRACLES

*"For I will not presume to speak of anything except what Christ
has accomplished through me, resulting in the obedience of the Gentiles by word and deed,
in the power of signs and wonders, in the power of the Spirit."*
—Romans 15:18–19

I. THE GIFT OF WORKINGS OF MIRACLES DEFINED

Miracles include supernatural healings, but they go beyond healings to encompass other supernatural phenomena, such as unusual meteorological happenings. We can best begin to understand the gift by exploring what a variety of Bible teachers (listed alphabetically) have said about it:

A.   Kenneth Hagin (late father of the Word of Faith movement)

The gift of the workings of miracles is the supernatural intervention of God in the ordinary course of nature, a temporary suspension of the accustomed order, or an interruption of the system of nature as we know it, operated by the power of the Holy Spirit.... The difference between the gift of faith and the workings of miracles is that the gift of faith *receives* a miracle and the working of miracles *works* a miracle.... [As evangelist Howard Carter explained,] this working of miracles "is indeed a mighty gift, glorifying the God of all power...stimulating the faith of His people and astonishing and confounding the unbelief of the wicked."[1]

B.   Dick Iverson (author, founding pastor of City Bible Church [Oregon], formerly called Portland Bible Temple)

> A miracle is a happening or event which is supernatural; the performance of something which is against the laws of nature…. Miracles defy reason and transcend natural laws.

> …The gift of miracles is simply the God-given ability to cooperate with God as He performs miracles. It is actually a co-action, or a joint operation; man participating with God in the performing of the impossible. It is not man performing miracles, but God performing miracles through a cooperative act with men.[2]

C.   Derek Prince (late author, international Bible teacher)

> A healing…is often imperceptible to the senses…[but] a miracle is usually perceptible to the senses and almost instantaneous, and it produces a change that goes beyond healing.…

> This gift is more properly designated as the double plural "workings of miracles." Moreover, Paul wrote about workings of miracles three times—in the tenth and twenty-eighth verses of 1 Corinthians 12 and in the fifth verse of Galatians 3. The Greek word translated "*miracles*" in these verses is the plural form of *dunamis*. *Dunamis* means "power," and therefore, translated literally, the gift would be "workings of powers." These workings refer to the God-given ability to demonstrate the supernatural power of the Holy Spirit at work.…

> If you study the miracles in Scripture, you will find that almost every time, an act of faith triggered them. Sometimes, it was a very simple act.

> In one way, healings merge with miracles; an instantaneous, visible healing is a miracle. In another way, miracles merge with faith.[3]

D.   David Pytches (Anglican bishop, author)

> The gift of miraculous powers operates through individual persons by the supernatural intervention of the Holy Spirit in the natural order…. Miracles vindicate the name of God and the gospel, and cause all those who witness them to reflect.[4]

E.   Sam Storms (author, Bible teacher, former visiting associate professor of theology at Wheaton College)

> The word often translated "miracles" in 1 Corinthians 12:10 is actually the Greek word for powers (*dunamis*). Thus we again have a double plural, "workings of powers," which probably points to a certain variety in these operations.

[They are] "workings" or "effectings" or "productions" of "powers" [of the Holy Spirit].…

[Theologian Wayne Grudem defines a miracle as] "a less common kind of God's activity in which he arouses people's awe and wonder and bears witness to himself."… The God who is always and everywhere present, upholding and sustaining and directing all things to their appointed consummation, is now working in a surprising and unfamiliar way.[5]

F. Peter Wagner (missiologist, author, apostolic teacher)

The gift of miracles is the special ability that God gives to certain members of the body of Christ to serve as human intermediaries through whom it pleases God to perform powerful acts that are perceived by observers to have altered the ordinary course of nature (see Acts 9:36–42; 19:11–20; 20:7–12; Rom. 15:18–19; 1 Cor. 12:10, 28; 2 Cor. 12:12).[6]

G. John Wimber (late author, international Vineyard leader)

[The results of the gift of the workings of miracles] are events in which people and things are beneficially affected by an extraordinary power of God working through an individual.[7]

II. QUALITIES AND EXAMPLES OF WORKINGS OF MIRACLES

A. Miracles Disregard the Laws of Nature

Healings can sometimes be spectacular, but miracles are even more impressive. One reason is that miracles appear to disregard the laws of nature. For example, no matter what kind of water or jars you might use, you could never change plain water into fine wine by any natural process:

Nearby stood six stone water jars, the kind used by the Jews for ceremonial washing, each holding from twenty to thirty gallons. Jesus said to the servants, "Fill the jars with water"; so they filled them to the brim. Then he told them, "Now draw some out and take it to the master of the banquet." They did so, and the master of the banquet tasted the water that had been turned into wine. He did not realize where it had come from, though the servants who had drawn the water knew. Then he called the bridegroom aside and said, "Everyone brings out the choice wine first and then the cheaper wine after the guests have had too much to drink; but you have saved the best till now." What Jesus did here in Cana of Galilee was the first of the signs through which he revealed his glory; and his disciples believed in him. (John 2:6–11 NIV)

B.   Miracles (Signs and Wonders) Can Result in Salvation

God would probably not perform a miracle randomly or away from human notice, because miracles are meant to seize people's attention and to show that God is real and relevant. There is no guarantee that the people will turn wholeheartedly to Him as a result, but they will be forced to think about Him and will be much more inclined toward belief. That's the effect miracles had on the Samaritan magician named Simon who followed Philip around:

> *Even Simon himself believed; and after being baptized, he continued on with Philip, and as he observed signs and great miracles taking place, he was constantly amazed.*

(Acts 8:13)

C.   Miracles Can Provide Protection and Deliverance from Perils

> *As Pharaoh drew near, the sons of Israel looked, and behold, the Egyptians were marching after them, and they became very frightened; so the sons of Israel cried out to the LORD. Then they said to Moses, "Is it because there were no graves in Egypt that you have taken us away to die in the wilderness? Why have you dealt with us in this way, bringing us out of Egypt? Is this not the word that we spoke to you in Egypt, saying, 'Leave us alone that we may serve the Egyptians'? For it would have been better for us to serve the Egyptians than to die in the wilderness." But Moses said to the people, "Do not fear! Stand by and see the salvation of the LORD which He will accomplish for you today; for the Egyptians whom you have seen today, you will never see them again forever. The LORD will fight for you while you keep silent." Then the LORD said to Moses, "Why are you crying out to Me? Tell the sons of Israel to go forward. As for you, lift up your staff and stretch out your hand over the sea and divide it, and the sons of Israel shall go through the midst of the sea on dry land.... Then Moses stretched out his hand over the sea; and the LORD swept the sea back by a strong east wind all night and turned the sea into dry land, so the waters were divided. The sons of Israel went through the midst of the sea on the dry land, and the waters were like a wall to them on their right hand and on their left. Then the Egyptians took up the pursuit, and all Pharaoh's horses, his chariots and his horsemen went in after them into the midst of the sea. At the morning watch, the LORD looked down on the army of the Egyptians through the pillar of fire and cloud and brought the army of the Egyptians into confusion. He caused their chariot wheels to swerve, and He made them drive with difficulty; so the Egyptians said, "Let us flee from Israel, for the LORD is fighting for them against the Egyptians." Then the LORD said to Moses, "Stretch out your hand over the sea so that the waters may come back over the Egyptians, over their chariots and their horsemen." So Moses stretched out his hand over the sea, and the sea returned to its normal state at daybreak, while the Egyptians were fleeing right into it; then the Lord overthrew the Egyptians in the midst of the sea. The waters returned and covered the chariots and the horsemen, even Pharaoh's entire army that had gone into the sea after them; not even one of them remained. But the sons of Israel walked on dry land through the midst of the sea, and*

*the waters were like a wall to them on their right hand and on their left. Thus the LORD
saved Israel that day from the hand of the Egyptians, and Israel saw the Egyptians dead
on the seashore. When Israel saw the great power which the LORD had used against
the Egyptians, the people feared the LORD, and they believed in the LORD and in His
servant Moses.* (Exodus 14:10–16, 21–31)

III. HOW MIRACLES OCCUR: THE WILL OF GOD PLUS HUMAN OBEDIENCE

A. By Hearing the Word of God

Miracles are almost always sparked by someone's simple act of obedience. When God part-
ed the Red Sea for the Israelites, Moses' job was not strenuous. God told him to lift up his staff
and stretch out his hand over the sea. (See Exodus 14:16.) Later, when Moses and the people
arrived at Marah where the waters were too bitter to drink, the Lord told Moses to throw a
particular tree into the pool of water, and by a miracle the water became sweet. (See Exodus
15:23–25.) In both cases, Moses had to follow through. Neither the staff nor the tree caused
the miracle; the miracle was effected by the power of God. But Moses had to obey explicitly.
If he had shouted at the sea instead of raising his staff over it, it's quite possible that the Egyptians would have caught up with them. If he had slipped the tree into the water quietly (or if
he had tossed in his staff as a substitute) instead of throwing the designated tree in with a big
splash, the Israelites' drinking water would most likely have remained bitter.

Likewise, when the Spirit directed the prophet Ezekiel to the valley of the dry bones, He
instructed the prophet what to say and do, and Ezekiel acted upon those instructions, obeying
explicitly. (See Ezekiel 37:1–10.)

Obedience is not an experiment. It is a real commitment, and it may involve performing a
seemingly ridiculous act in front of multitudes of people.

B. By Believing the Word

Moses and Ezekiel believed the words God told them. Obedience is preceded by a communication from God. Obedient faith comes from hearing: *"So faith comes from hearing, and
hearing by the word of Christ"* (Romans 10:17).

In another example, the Lord told the prophet Elijah to give a destitute widow an unlike-
ly-sounding word of direction, but her small supply of oil multiplied to fill every last jar she
had collected in obedience to that word. (See 2 Kings 4:1–7.) Miracles occur when we believe
and act on the word of the Lord. (See also Mark 11:23; Acts 13:9–12.)

C. By Speaking the Word

God is the only *uncreated* Being in the universe, having created everything else that has ever
existed: *"By the word of the LORD the heavens were made, and by the breath of His mouth all their
host"* (Psalm 33:6).

God the Son—the Word made flesh—*"upholds all things by the word [rhema, Greek] of His power"* (Hebrews 1:3; see also, for example, John 5:8; John 11:43–44; Acts 3:5–7). He upholds all things by the *rhema*, or spoken word, that He utters.

D.   By Acting on the Word

1.   Unless obedient acts of faith accompany the spoken word of the Lord, nothing can happen:

> *So faith by itself, if it has no works, is dead.*   (James 2:17 NRSV)

2.   The only way the mountain can be cast into the sea is by faith—faith that stands firm, without a flicker of doubt:

> *Truly I say to you, whoever says to this mountain, "Be taken up and cast into the sea," and does not doubt in his heart, but believes that what he says is going to happen, it will be granted him.*   (Mark 11:23)

3.   Paul acted in faith to effect miracles. When Eutychus fell from a high window and died, Paul hurried down to where he lay, *"fell on him,"* and embraced him, resulting in a resurrection miracle:

> *And in a window sat a certain young man named Eutychus, who was sinking into a deep sleep. He was overcome by sleep; and as Paul continued speaking, he fell down from the third story and was taken up dead. But Paul went down, fell on him, and embracing him said, "Do not trouble yourselves, for his life is in him."*   (Acts 20:9–10 NKJV)

IV. THE GRAND PURPOSE OF MIRACLES

God's grand purpose is to build up His kingdom. The following are several ways He has used miracles to do this:

A.   Delivering and Preserving His People

1.   The miracles and plagues in Egypt were for the deliverance and preservation of Israel as an entire people.

2.   This purpose of deliverance and preservation is also true on an individual basis:

> *When they came to the Jordan, they cut down trees. But as one was felling a log, his ax head fell into the water; he cried out, "Alas, master! It was borrowed." Then the man of God [Elisha] said, "Where did it fall?" When he showed him the place, he cut off a stick, and threw it in there, and made the iron float. He said, "Pick it up." So he reached out his hand and took it.*
> (2 Kings 6:4–7 NRSV)

> *While He was still speaking, they came from the house of the synagogue official, saying, "Your daughter has died; why trouble the Teacher anymore?" But Jesus, overhearing what was being spoken, said to the synagogue official, "Do not be afraid any longer, only believe." And He allowed no one to accompany Him, except Peter and James and John the brother of James. They came to the house of the synagogue official; and He saw a commotion, and people loudly weeping and wailing. And entering in, He said to them, "Why make a commotion and weep? The child has not died, but is asleep." They began laughing at Him. But putting them all out, He took along the child's father and mother and His own companions, and entered the room where the child was. Taking the child by the hand, He said to her, "Talitha kum!" (which translated means, "Little girl, I say to you, get up!"). Immediately the girl got up and began to walk, for she was twelve years old. And immediately they were completely astounded.* (Mark 5:35–42)

B. Building Up the Faith of Believers

God builds up the people who populate His kingdom, and He exalts His glory through miraculous works so that more people will come to believe in Him and follow Him.

1. *"What Jesus did here in Cana of Galilee was the first of the signs through which he revealed his glory; and his disciples **believed** in him"* (John 2:11 NIV).

2. *"Many other signs Jesus also performed in the presence of the disciples, which are not written in this book; but these have been written so that you may **believe** that Jesus is the Christ, the Son of God; and that **believing** you may have life in His name"* (John 20:30–31).

C. Confirming the Preaching of the Word of God

1. Miracles are meant to accompany the preaching of the gospel, working in connection with evangelism to confirm the work of the cross of Jesus and the power of the Word of God. This is the thrust of the Great Commission:

   > *And [Jesus] said to them, "Go into all the world and preach the gospel to all creation. He who has believed and has been baptized shall be saved; but he who has disbelieved shall be condemned. These signs will accompany those who have believed: in My name they will cast out demons, they will speak with new tongues; they will pick up serpents, and if they drink any deadly poison, it will not hurt them; they will lay hands on the sick, and they will recover." So then, when the Lord Jesus had spoken to them, He was received up into heaven and sat down at the right hand of God. And they went out and preached everywhere, while the Lord worked with them, and confirmed the word by the signs that followed.* (Mark 16:15–20)

2. Jesus has made us co-laborers with Him by the miracle-working power of His Holy Spirit. Jesus does not hoard all of the excitement; to this day, He wants His disciples to see miracles and to be the avenue of His miracle-working power in the earth:

> *Truly, truly, I say to you, he who believes in Me, the works that I do, he will do also; and greater works than these he will do; because I go to the Father. Whatever you ask in My name, that will I do, so that the Father may be glorified in the Son.* (John 14:12–13)

3. As Jesus said,

> *All things are possible to him who believes.* (Mark 9:23)

LESSON NINE: THE WORKINGS OF MIRACLES

(Answers to these questions can be found in the back of the study guide.)

Fill in the Blank

1. In your own words, define the gift of workings of miracles:

   _____

   _____

   _____

2. Miracles are almost always sparked by someone's simple act of _____.

3. "The Greek word translated *'miracles'*...is the plural form of *dunamis. Dunamis* means

   '_____,' and therefore, translated literally, the gift would be '_____

   ___ _____.'"

Multiple Choice—Choose the best answer from the list below:

A—preaching	C—love
B—training	D—faith

4. Unless obedient acts of _____ accompany the spoken word of the Lord, nothing can happen.

5. Miracles are meant to accompany the _____ of the gospel, working in connection with evangelism to confirm the work of the cross of Jesus and the power of the Word of God.

True or False

6. Only certain especially gifted believers in the body of Christ can expect to be used to perform miracles.   **T / F**

7. Miracles appear to disregard the laws of nature.   **T / F**

8. Hearing, believing, speaking, and acting—all these help to release a miracle.   **T / F**

Scripture Memorization

Write out and memorize Hebrews 2:1–4. This passage is from the *New American Standard Version*; choose another version if you prefer:

> *For this reason we must pay much closer attention to what we have heard, so that we do not drift away from it. For if the word spoken through angels proved unalterable, and every transgression and disobedience received a just penalty, how will we escape if we neglect so great a salvation? After it was at the first spoken through the Lord, it was confirmed to us by those who heard, God also testifying with them, both by signs and wonders and by various miracles and by gifts of the Holy Spirit according to His own will.*

VOCAL GIFTS—THE GIFTS THAT SPEAK

"There are varieties of gifts, but the same Spirit. And there are varieties of ministries, and the same Lord. There are varieties of effects, but the same God who works all things in all persons. But to each one is given the manifestation of the Spirit for the common good."
—1 Corinthians 12:4–7

In order to truly partner with God in His work, believers must be able to speak with His insight and authority. Verbal gifts communicate His will to the church and to the world (as well as to the forces of darkness). The gift of various kinds of tongues (languages)—received in a dialect that is almost always unknown to both speaker and listener—goes alongside the gift of interpretation of tongues, so that people can understand the message in their own language. The gift of prophecy, like the gift of discernment, can be received through any of the five senses and is released for the encouragement and edification of others.

Lesson Ten

THE GIFT OF VARIOUS KINDS OF TONGUES

"Men of Judea and all you who live in Jerusalem, let this be known to you and give heed to my words. For these men are not drunk, as you suppose, for it is only the third hour of the day; but this is what was spoken of through the prophet Joel: 'And it shall be in the last days,' God says, 'that I will pour forth of My Spirit on all mankind….'"
—Acts 2:14–17

I. THE GIFT OF VARIOUS KINDS OF TONGUES DEFINED

Tongues is a gift for all believers. Just as every believer is meant to be filled with the Holy Spirit, so every believer has the option of praying or speaking in tongues. Our panel of Bible teachers (listed in alphabetical order) explore what the gift means:

A. Kenneth Hagin (late father of the Word of Faith movement)

Diverse kinds of tongues is supernatural utterance by the Holy Spirit in languages never learned by the speaker nor understood by the speaker, nor necessarily always understood by the hearer. Speaking with tongues has nothing whatsoever to do with linguistic ability; it has nothing to do with the mind or the intellect of the man. It is a vocal miracle of the Holy Spirit.[1]

B. Dick Iverson (author, founding pastor of City Bible Church [Oregon], formerly called Portland Bible Temple)

The gift of tongues is the God-given enablement to communicate in a language one does not know….

106

...This is a *"manifestation of the Spirit"* (1 Corinthians 12:7), and not human ability. It has absolutely nothing to do with natural linguistic ability, eloquence of speech, or a new sanctified way of talking.... The gift of tongues is a supernatural manifestation or expression of the Holy Spirit through a person's speech organs. It is a direct manifestation of the miraculous.[2]

C. Derek Prince (late author, international Bible teacher)

[The gift of tongues] is the ability given by the Holy Spirit to speak in a language not understood by the speaker. [It] is plural in both its aspects, and it is set in the public assembly for ministry to that assembly.[3]

D. David Pytches (Anglican bishop, author)

[The gift of tongues] is spontaneous inspired utterance by the Holy Spirit, where the normal voice organs are used, but the conscious mind plays no part. The languages spoken or sung are entirely unlearned by the speaker.[4]

E. Sam Storms (author, Bible teacher, former visiting associate professor of theology at Wheaton College)

Tongues are neither God's greatest gift to his most highly favored children, nor the devil's most sinister tool of deceit. Tongues are just like any other gift of the Spirit. It is not a sign of God's special love. It is not a sign of heightened maturity in Christ. It is not a sign of superior zeal or commitment.... In fact, *tongues are not a sign of anything.* They are merely one among many of what the apostle Paul calls "manifestation of the Spirit" (1 Cor. 12:7) given to believers for the common good of the Church.[5]

F. Peter Wagner (missiologist, author, apostolic teacher)

The gift of tongues is the special ability that God gives to certain members of the Body of Christ to (1) speak to God in a language they have never learned and/or (2) receive and communicate an immediate message from God to His people through a divinely anointed utterance in a language they have never learned (see Mark 16:17; Acts 2:1–13; 10:44–46; 19:1–7; 1 Cor. 12:10, 28; 14:13–19).[6]

G. John Wimber (late author, international Vineyard leader)

Various kinds of tongues are Spirit-inspired, spontaneous utterances in which the conscious mind plays no part. The gift of tongues is speaking in a language (either earthly or angelic) that the speaker has never learned or understood. This is practiced privately by a believer and may be used at will for his own edification. The gift of tongues is also used in public as an ecstatic utterance following an anointing from God.[7]

II. SCRIPTURES ABOUT THE GIFT OF VARIOUS KINDS OF TONGUES

A. Tongues in the Early Church

The following Scriptures show that people in the early church spoke in tongues when they received the Holy Spirit. This gives us a biblical basis to expect God to do the same with us today:

> *And they were all filled with the Holy Spirit and began to speak with other tongues, as the Spirit was giving them utterance. Now there were Jews living in Jerusalem, devout men from every nation under heaven. And when this sound occurred, the crowd came together, and were bewildered because each one of them was hearing them speak in his own language.* (Acts 2:4–6)

> *All the circumcised believers who came with Peter were amazed, because the gift of the Holy Spirit had been poured out on the Gentiles also. For they were hearing them speaking with tongues and exalting God. Then Peter answered, "Surely no one can refuse the water for these to be baptized who have received the Holy Spirit just as we did, can he?" And he ordered them to be baptized in the name of Jesus Christ.* (Acts 10:45–48)

> *It happened that while Apollos was at Corinth, Paul passed through the upper country and came to Ephesus, and found some disciples. He said to them, "Did you receive the Holy Spirit when you believed?" And they said to him, "No, we have not even heard whether there is a Holy Spirit." And he said, "Into what then were you baptized?" And they said, "Into John's baptism." Paul said, "John baptized with the baptism of repentance, telling the people to believe in Him who was coming after him, that is, in Jesus." When they heard this, they were baptized in the name of the Lord Jesus. And when Paul had laid his hands upon them, the Holy Spirit came on them, and they began speaking with tongues and prophesying.* (Acts 19:1–6)

B. Tongues for Personal Communion with God

The gift of tongues can be used for personal communion with God on a continual basis. That's why Jude endorsed the use of the gift of tongues, which he called "praying in the Spirit": "*But you, beloved, build yourselves up on your most holy faith; pray in the Holy Spirit*" (Jude 1:20 NRSV).

This vital gift leads to a great increase of revelation in the life of the believer.

Likewise the Spirit helps us in our weakness; for we do not know how to pray as we ought, but that very Spirit intercedes with sighs [many other translations use "groans" or "groanings"] too deep for words. And God, who searches the heart, knows what is the mind of the Spirit, because the Spirit intercedes for the saints according to the will of God.   (Romans 8:26–27 NRSV)

Someone who speaks in tongues is praying, and praying in this way builds the person up. *"One who speaks in a tongue does not speak to men but to God…. One who speaks in a tongue edifies himself"* (1 Corinthians 14:2, 4).

III. PURPOSES OF DIFFERENT KINDS OF TONGUES

A.   For Praise to God

And the believers from among the circumcised who had come with Peter were amazed, because the gift of the Holy Spirit was poured out even on the Gentiles. For they were hearing them speaking in tongues and extolling God.   (Acts 10:45–46 ESV)

B.   For Intercession

Prayer in tongues can be on behalf of an individual, a group of people, or a situation. This usage does not require an interpretation, because it is prayer that God understands, even if the words are a mystery to the people speaking (or listening).

C.   To Rebuke the Powers of Darkness

The Lord often uses such prayer to rebuke the forces of darkness, who can comprehend the supernatural reproofs even when the speakers cannot. Surely, in such cases, the victory is often won by a combination of prayer in tongues and the gifts of faith and discernment.

D.   For Exhortation, Edification, and Comfort

The gift of tongues, when used with the gift of interpretation of tongues, can be the means of bringing exhortation, edification, and comfort to a group or to an individual. This operation can equal the gift of prophecy in its impact. (See 1 Corinthians 14:3–5.)

E.   For a Sign for Unbelievers

"So then tongues are for a sign, not to those who believe but to unbelievers" (1 Corinthians 14:22; see the rest of chapter 14 for Paul's full discussion of the public use of the gift). God sometimes uses the gift of tongues as a sign of His glorious presence in an assembly, which can be particularly powerful as a sign to unbelievers. Used in this way, the gift has proven to be very effective on the mission field for convincing those who do not yet believe in God.

IV. GUIDELINES FOR USING THE GIFT OF TONGUES

A. Private and Public Tongues

In his first letter to the Corinthians, Paul wrote very detailed guidelines for speaking in tongues, both in private settings and in church meetings, and his advice was not meant only for the church in Corinth. He acknowledged that not everyone who exercises a tongue in private communion with God will also exercise the public ministry of tongues. (See 1 Corinthians 12:29–30.)

B. Combination of Tongues and Interpretation

Paul also indicated that in a public assembly, it is out of place to speak out loud in a tongue without being prompted by God's special leading and without supplying the interpretation:

> I thank God, I speak in tongues more than you all; however, in the church I desire to speak five words with my mind so that I may instruct others also, rather than ten thousand words in a tongue.… If anyone speaks in a tongue, it should be by two or at the most three, and each in turn, and one must interpret; but if there is no interpreter, he must keep silent in the church; and let him speak to himself and to God.
>
> (1 Corinthians 14:18–19, 27–28)

C. Praying in Tongues

It's perfectly okay to pray in tongues to yourself in a church setting; that's not forbidden at all. But utterances in tongues don't benefit anybody in attendance unless they can be interpreted into a commonly understood language.

> If there is no one to interpret, let each of them keep silent in church and speak to himself and to God.
>
> (1 Corinthians 14:28 ESV)

V. SCRIPTURAL REASONS WHY BELIEVERS SHOULD SPEAK IN TONGUES

A. They Are a Sign of the Resurrection

Utterances in unknown tongues signify that the resurrection of Jesus Christ really happened—that He is risen and glorified. Peter said to the awed unbelievers on the day of Pentecost,

> Therefore having been exalted to the right hand of God, and having received from the Father the promise of the Holy Spirit, [Jesus] has poured forth this which you both see and hear.
>
> (Acts 2:33)

B.   They Are an Acknowledgment of Personal Acceptance of Jesus' Lordship

The gift of tongues is a sign of one's yieldedness to God because speaking in tongues involves surrendering to Him our most *"unruly"* member, the tongue:

> *For we all stumble in many things. If anyone does not stumble in word, he is a perfect man, able also to bridle the whole body. Indeed, we put bits in horses' mouths that they may obey us, and we turn their whole body. Look also at ships: although they are so large and are driven by fierce winds, they are turned by a very small rudder wherever the pilot desires. Even so the tongue is a little member and boasts great things. See how great a forest a little fire kindles! And the tongue is a fire, a world of iniquity. The tongue is so set among our members that it defiles the whole body, and sets on fire the course of nature; and it is set on fire by hell. For every kind of beast and bird, of reptile and creature of the sea, is tamed and has been tamed by mankind. But no man can tame the tongue. It is an unruly evil, full of deadly poison.* (James 3:2–8 NKJV)

C.   They Are a Sign of Repentance

Since the day of Pentecost, speaking in tongues has proved to be a sign of repentance and of reception of the Spirit:

> *Now when they heard this* [the message of salvation], *they were pierced to the heart, and said to Peter and the rest of the apostles, "Brethren, what shall we do?" Peter said to them, "Repent, and each of you be baptized in the name of Jesus Christ for the forgiveness of your sins; and you will receive the gift of the Holy Spirit."* (Acts 2:37–38; see also Acts 10:46–47)

D.   They Are a Tool to Deal with Pride

One must become humble and childlike in order to speak to God in tongues, abandoning self-determination and self-sufficiency. (See, for example, 1 Corinthians 1:18–31; Matthew 18:2–5.) In an ongoing way, the gift of tongues succeeds in keeping pride at bay.

E.   They Allow God to Speak Supernaturally to Humanity

See, for example, 1 Corinthians 12:7, 10; 14:5, 13–22.

F.   They Allow Us to Speak to God

The gift of tongues enables us to speak to God in both worship and intercessory prayer. See 1 Corinthians 14:2, 15–18; Acts 2:11; 10:45–46.

G.   They Bring Edification

Praying in tongues (praying "in the Spirit") is one of the most strategic ways to build up one's faith. See 1 Corinthians 14:4, 15–16; Jude 20; Ephesians 6:18.

H. They Are a Sign to Unbelievers

When unbelievers hear believers speaking in tongues, they are exposed to the reality that God is alive and is personally involved in people's lives. See 1 Corinthians 14:22.

I. They Are the Fulfillment of Prophecy

The gift of tongues fulfills biblical prophecy:

> *With foreign lips and strange tongues God will speak to this people.*
>
> (Isaiah 28:11 NIV)

J. They Fulfill Biblical Expectation for the Believer

Speaking in tongues is a normal and expected sign of the Spirit's indwelling in a believer in Christ.

> *You will receive power when the Holy Spirit comes on you; and you will be my witnesses in Jerusalem, and in all Judea and Samaria, and to the ends of the earth.*
>
> (Acts 1:8 NIV)

> *When Paul had laid his hands on them, the Holy Spirit came on them, and they began speaking in tongues and prophesying.*
>
> (Acts 19:6 ESV; see also Mark 16:17; John 7:38–39)

K. They Can Enhance Evangelism

As on the day of Pentecost, public speaking in tongues can enhance evangelism:

> *Amazed and astonished, they asked, "Are not all these who are speaking Galileans? And how is it that we hear, each of us, in our own native language? Parthians, Medes, Elamites, and residents of Mesopotamia, Judea and Cappadocia, Pontus and Asia, Phrygia and Pamphylia, Egypt and the parts of Libya belonging to Cyrene, and visitors from Rome, both Jews and proselytes, Cretans and Arabs—in our own languages we hear them speaking about God's deeds of power."… So those who welcomed his message were baptized, and that day about three thousand persons were added. They devoted themselves to the apostles' teaching and fellowship, to the breaking of bread and the prayers.*
>
> (Acts 2:7–11, 41–42 NRSV)

LESSON TEN: THE GIFT OF VARIOUS KINDS OF TONGUES

(Answers to these questions can be found in the back of the study guide.)

Fill in the Blank

1. In your own words, define the gift of various kinds of tongues:

    _____

    _____

    _____

2. List at least three of the purposes of the gift of various kinds of tongues:

    (a) _____

    (b) _____

    (c) _____

3. One must become humble and childlike in order to speak to God in tongues, abandoning self-determination and _____. In an ongoing way, the gift of tongues succeeds in keeping _____ at bay.

113

Multiple Choice—Choose the best answer from the list below:

A—acknowledgment   C—manifestation

B—expression   D—utterance

4. The gift of tongues is a(n) "'_____ *of the Spirit*' (1 Corinthians 12:7), and not human ability."

5. "[The gift of tongues] is spontaneous inspired _____ by the Holy Spirit."

True or False

6. In a public setting, it can sometimes be all right to speak out loud in tongues without an interpretation.   **T / F**

7. The gift of tongues is never a positive sign for an unbeliever.   **T / F**

8. When a believer speaks in tongues, he or she is speaking to God.   **T / F**

Scripture Memorization

Write out and memorize Acts 2:14–20, which includes a quotation from Joel 2:28–32. The following passage is from the *New King James Version*. However, choose the Scripture version that is most familiar to you; it will help with memorizing this lengthier passage.

> *But Peter, standing up with the eleven, raised his voice and said to them, "Men of Judea and all who dwell in Jerusalem, let this be known to you, and heed my words. For these are not drunk, as you suppose, since it is only the third hour of the day. But this is what was spoken by the prophet Joel: 'And it shall come to pass in the last days, says God, that I will pour out of My Spirit on all flesh; your sons and your daughters shall prophesy, your young men shall see visions, your old men shall dream dreams. And on My menservants and on My maidservants I will pour out My Spirit in those days; and they shall prophesy. I will show wonders in heaven above and signs in the earth beneath: blood and fire and vapor of smoke. The sun shall be turned into darkness, and the moon into blood, before the coming of the great and awesome day of the LORD.'"*

Lesson Eleven

THE GIFT OF INTERPRETATION OF TONGUES

"Pursue love and strive for the spiritual gifts…. Now, brothers and sisters, if I come to you speaking in tongues, how will I benefit you unless I speak to you in some revelation or knowledge or prophecy or teaching? It is the same way with lifeless instruments that produce sound, such as the flute or the harp. If they do not give distinct notes, how will anyone know what is being played? And if the bugle gives an indistinct sound, who will get ready for battle? So with yourselves; if in a tongue you utter speech that is not intelligible, how will anyone know what is being said? For you will be speaking into the air. There are doubtless many different kinds of sounds in the world, and nothing is without sound. If then I do not know the meaning of a sound, I will be a foreigner to the speaker and the speaker a foreigner to me. So with yourselves; since you are eager for spiritual gifts, strive to excel in them for building up the church. Therefore, one who speaks in a tongue should pray for the power to interpret."
—1 Corinthians 14:1, 6–13 (NRSV)

I. THE GIFT OF INTERPRETATION OF TONGUES DEFINED

Manifestations of the other seven primary gifts of the Spirit appeared in the Old Testament, but the gifts of tongues and interpretation of tongues do not seem to be mentioned by earlier writers except to be prophesied about. Paul made the connection when he quoted from Isaiah 28:11–12 in his instruction about tongues to the church in Corinth:

In the Law it is written: "With other tongues and through the lips of foreigners I will speak to this people, but even then they will not listen to me, says the Lord."

(1 Corinthians 14:21 NIV)

115

The gift of the interpretation of tongues (defined below by various Bible teachers) is therefore distinct to Christianity since the day of Pentecost, alongside the gift of tongues.

A. Kenneth Hagin (late father of the Word of Faith movement)

The [gift of] interpretation of tongues is *the supernatural showing-forth by the Spirit of the meaning of an utterance in other tongues....* It is not a *translation* of the unknown tongue; it is the *interpretation* of tongues.... It depends upon another gift—divers kinds of tongues—to operate.... The purpose of [this gift] is to render the gift of tongues understandable to the hearers so that the whole church congregation, as well as the one who gave the utterance in an unknown tongue, may know what has been said and may be edified thereby.[1]

B. Dick Iverson (author, founding pastor of City Bible Church [Oregon], formerly called Portland Bible Temple)

The gift of interpretation is the supernatural, spontaneous ability to interpret a communication given in tongues into the language understood by the people present. Again, it has absolutely nothing to do with natural knowledge of languages, but comes directly from the Holy Spirit.[2]

C. Derek Prince (late author, international Bible teacher)

The gift of interpretation of tongues...[is] the ability given to a believer by the Holy Spirit to speak, in a language understood by the speaker, the meaning of words previously spoken in an unknown language....

Interpretation must not necessarily be understood to mean a word-for-word translation, but rather a rendering of the general sense of what was spoken in the tongue.[3]

D. David Pytches (Anglican bishop, author)

The gift of interpretation of tongues is a supernatural revelation through the Holy Spirit which enables the Christian believer to communicate in the language of the listeners the dynamic equivalent of that which was spoken "in tongues."[4]

E. Sam Storms (author, Bible teacher, former visiting associate professor of theology at Wheaton College)

The charisma [gift] of interpretation of tongues is the Spirit-empowered ability to translate a public utterance of tongues into the language of the congregation....

The interpretation of tongues may be the most neglected gift in the Body of Christ. It is also one of the more important gifts, insofar as it alone makes possible the introduction of tongues-speech and its obvious blessings into the gathered assembly of believers.[5]

F.   Peter Wagner (missiologist, author, apostolic teacher)

The gift of interpretation of tongues is the special ability that God gives to certain members of the Body of Christ to make known in the vernacular the message of one who speaks in tongues (see 1 Cor. 12:10, 30; 14:13, 26–28).[6]

G.   John Wimber (late author, international Vineyard leader)

The gift of the interpretation of tongues is the God-given inspiration to speak in the language of the listeners, giving to them the dynamic equivalent of that which was spoken by the speaker in tongues. It is not a translation. Both tongues and interpretation may be spoken or given in a song.[7]

II. GUIDELINES FOR INTERPRETATION OF TONGUES

A.   "Diversities of Activities"

First Corinthians 12:4–6 states:

There are diversities of gifts, but the same Spirit. There are differences of ministries, but the same Lord. And there are diversities of activities, but it is the same God who works all in all.   (NKJV)

The phrase *"diversities of activities"* is translated as *"different kinds of working"* in the *New International Version*. Where the gift of interpretation of tongues is concerned, this means that the gift operates quite differently through different believers. For some people, an interpretation comes to mind as just one introductory phrase, and they must "launch out in faith" before they receive the rest, while others hear words and whole sentences in their minds, or see words displayed on a scroll or a screen in their mind's eye. Still others receive visions that they go on to relate in their own words; or, a general thought may drop into their minds, which they "clothe with words of their own choosing," as the Holy Spirit leads them. Every mode of operation depends on faith to a significant degree.[8]

The gifts of tongues and interpretation of tongues can be more than what we're used to in our gatherings where tongues and interpretation occur. When someone speaks a message in a tongue and then, after a gap of maybe fifteen seconds, somebody speaks out the interpretation, that is valid enough; but it is only one application of the gift of interpretation of tongues. Keeping ourselves to that one application seems to limit the free moving of the Holy Spirit.

Oral Roberts used to take people on tours of Oral Roberts University, and he would say, "You see all of this? All of this was built by praying in tongues." He explained that he got the vision for every building by praying in tongues and then interpreting his own tongues back to himself. In fact, he recommended that people learn to do that by praying in tongues for five minutes, and then stopping and speaking in their native language, which he taught would either be an interpretation of the mystery the person had just uttered in tongues or a prophetic prayer, both of which would be beneficial to receive.

B. Tongues plus Interpretation Is Equivalent to Prophetic Exhortation

An exhortation in tongues, when interpreted, is like a prophetic exhortation in the language of the hearers. It accomplishes the same purpose—edifying the church—and should be evaluated by the same standards:

> *I wish you all spoke with tongues, but even more that you prophesied; for he who prophesies is greater than he who speaks with tongues, unless indeed he interprets, that the church may receive edification.* (1 Corinthians 14:5 NKJV)

(Kenneth Hagin used to say that if prophecy is like a dime, then tongues plus interpretation can often be like two nickels.) However, this equivalent of prophecy, which can be called an "exhorting tongue," or a "message tongue," is not the same as an uninterpreted "mystery tongue" used for personal devotions. Paul drew this contrast when he wrote,

> *For one who speaks in a tongue does not speak to men but to God; for no one understands, but in his spirit he speaks mysteries. But one who prophesies speaks to men for edification and exhortation and consolation. One who speaks in a tongue edifies himself; but one who prophesies edifies the church.* (1 Corinthians 14:2–4)

C. Praying to Receive Interpretation

A message in tongues and its interpretation do not necessarily need to come from two different people. If necessary, the person who delivers the message in tongues can pray to receive an interpretation and then speak aloud what he or she receives. In certain situations, this is not encouraged, but it may be the only way to obtain an interpretation in some cases, and it represents part of the *"diversities of activities"* carried by this gift:

> *Even so you, since you are zealous for spiritual gifts, let it be for the edification of the church that you seek to excel. Therefore let him who speaks in a tongue pray that he may interpret.* (1 Corinthians 14:12–13 NKJV)

D. Diversities of Tongues, Diversities of Interpretations

The key idea is diversity—an endless variety of languages and a limitless array of interpretations—as appointed and inspired by the Holy Spirit. In public situations, people do not speak out in tongues or interpretations whenever they wish, but only as they are led by the Spirit to do so. The orchestration is up to God.

Now there are varieties of gifts, but the same Spirit. And there are varieties of ministries, and the same Lord. There are varieties of effects, but the same God who works all things in all persons. But to each one is given the manifestation of the Spirit for the common good. For to one [and to another are given various gifts, including]…various kinds of tongues, and to another the interpretation of tongues. But one and the same Spirit works all these things, distributing to each one individually just as He wills.

(1 Corinthians 12:4–8, 10–11; see also Romans 12:3–8)

E.   In a Gathering, There Should Be Only Two or Three Messages in Tongues

Paul's guidelines for using tongues and interpretation in church gatherings apply to "message tongues" only, not to the personal use of the gift, in which the meaning of the words often remains a mystery:

If anyone speaks in a tongue, it should be by two or at the most three, and each in turn, and one must interpret; but if there is no interpreter, he must keep silent in the church; and let him speak to himself and to God. Let two or three prophets speak, and let the others pass judgment. But if a revelation is made to another who is seated, the first one must keep silent. For you can all prophesy one by one, so that all may learn and all may be exhorted; and the spirits of prophets are subject to prophets.

(1 Corinthians 14:27–32)

F.   Pray for This Gift of the Holy Spirit

Since there are always more tongues-speakers than there are people who can interpret a message in tongues, we have been invited to pray for this gift of interpretation:

Therefore, one who speaks in a tongue should pray for the power to interpret.

(1 Corinthians 14:13 NRSV)

Remember, this is a gift given by God, not something that we can study for as we might do in order to learn a foreign language. Interpretation of tongues is very much like the gift of prophecy, for which we are also invited to ask:

Pursue love, yet desire earnestly spiritual gifts, but especially that you may prophesy.

(1 Corinthians 14:1)

G.   Interpretation Is Not Exact Translation

Interpretation is not the same as word-for-word translation. If the message was sung, for instance, the interpretation may or may not be sung, too, and the tune may well be different. The interpretation is often longer or shorter than the message in tongues. The best scriptural example of this is Daniel's interpretation of the mysterious words *"Menē, menē, tekēl, upharsin"*—his interpretation was about nine times as long as the original message. (See Daniel 5:24–28.)

The interpretation may also step into another gift of the Spirit—prophecy—and continue on. Or there may be a prayer in tongues followed by a response from the Lord in prophecy.

There is so much diversity within the gifts of tongues and interpretation that only God can account for all the possibilities.

III. WHAT MESSAGES SHOULD BE INTERPRETED?

A. No Need to Interpret People's Initial Utterances at Their Spirit Baptism

There is no need to interpret the utterances in tongues that are spoken when people first receive the Holy Spirit. The New Testament does not record any interpretation on such occasions. That isn't to say that such tongues may not be understood. Recall that on the day of Pentecost, the outpouring of tongues among the believers in the upper room was actually comprehensible to the listeners in their (many) languages:

> *And they were all filled with the Holy Spirit and began to speak with other tongues, as the Spirit was giving them utterance. Now there were Jews living in Jerusalem, devout men from every nation under heaven. And when this sound occurred, the crowd came together, and were bewildered because each one of them was hearing them speak in his own language.* (Acts 2:4–6)

Likewise, when Peter preached to Cornelius' household, *"all the circumcised believers who came with Peter were amazed, because the gift of the Holy Spirit had been poured out on the Gentiles also. For they were hearing them speaking with tongues and exalting God"* (Acts 10:45–46).

B. When Not to Interpret

The New Testament indicates that when tongues are used for personal prayer or worship, they do not have to be interpreted, although there may be occasions in which they will be.

> *Likewise the Spirit helps us in our weakness. For we do not know what to pray for as we ought, but the Spirit himself intercedes for us with groanings too deep for words. And he who searches hearts knows what is the mind of the Spirit, because the Spirit intercedes for the saints according to the will of God.* (Romans 8:26–27 ESV)

> *For one who speaks in a tongue does not speak to men but to God; for no one understands, but in his spirit he speaks mysteries.* (1 Corinthians 14:2)

> *For if I pray in a tongue, my spirit prays, but my mind is unfruitful. So what shall I do? I will pray with my spirit, but I will also pray with my understanding; I will sing with my spirit, but I will also sing with my understanding. Otherwise when you are praising God in the Spirit, how can someone else, who is now put in the position of an inquirer, say "Amen" to your thanksgiving, since they do not know what you are saying? You are*

giving thanks well enough, but no one else is edified. I thank God that I speak in tongues more than all of you.   (1 Corinthians 14:14–18 NIV)

C.   When to Interpret

By and large, when audible tongues-speaking occurs in a public setting, it is meant to convey a message to the hearers and should be interpreted. The only tongues Paul said must have interpretation are such "message tongues."

The one who speaks in a tongue builds up himself, but the one who prophesies builds up the church.   (1 Corinthians 14:4 ESV)

Therefore, one who speaks in a tongue should pray for the power to interpret.
                                   (1 Corinthians 14:13 NRSV)

But if there is no interpreter, he must keep silent in the church; and let him speak to himself and to God.   (1 Corinthians 14:28)

D.   Sensitivity to the Holy Spirit

We need to try to grow in our sensitivity to God's voice for those times when a public message in tongues requires an interpretation. Ask yourself, "Is it my turn to exercise the gift? Am I 'getting something'?" It may be time to stand up and speak out.

Sensitivity to the Spirit's inner promptings is very important, and the learning process is more subjective than it is objective, because there is no list of absolute rules to go by. The Spirit's promptings are gentle (although He may move strongly for the sake of a beginner).

Be encouraged to ask the Spirit to build on your gift of tongues by granting you a gift of interpretation of tongues. Then keep stirring up the gift, learning something new from each occasion.

The gift of interpretation of tongues may be somewhat neglected today, but Paul did not neglect it, just as he did not neglect the gift of tongues. In fact, he listed these two gifts and discussed them much more often than he did many of the other gifts. Above all, he urged everyone to employ the gifts of the Spirit by means of the love of God. (See 1 Corinthians 13.)

LESSON ELEVEN: THE GIFT OF INTERPRETATION OF TONGUES

(Answers to these questions can be found in the back of the study guide.)

Fill in the Blank

1. In your own words, define the gift of interpretation of tongues:

    _____

    _____

    _____

    _____

2. "The gift of interpretation of tongues is a supernatural revelation through the Holy Spirit which enables the Christian believer to _____ in the language of the listeners the _____ _____ of that which was spoken 'in tongues.'"

3. "*Therefore, one who speaks in a tongue should pray for the power to _____*" (1 Corinthians 14:13 NRSV).

122

Multiple Choice—Choose the best answer from the list below:

A—tongues

C—compassionate

B—prophecy

D—sensitive

4.   Interpretation of tongues can be classified under the umbrella of _____.

5.   Learning to be _____ to the Spirit's inner promptings is all-important for using spiritual gifts, and this applies in a particular way to the gift of interpretation of tongues.

True or False

6.   Interpretation of a message spoken in tongues should be a direct translation of the unknown language.   **T / F**

7.   As a gift of the Spirit, interpretation of tongues follows certain absolute rules every time.   **T / F**

8.   When the gift of tongues is used in personal devotional times, no interpretation is required.   **T / F**

Scripture Memorization

To help you remember what you have learned about the gifts of the Spirit, write out and memorize Paul's classic listing of the nine gifts of the Spirit from 1 Corinthians 12:4–11. The following passage is from the *New American Standard Bible*; choose a different version if you prefer:

Now there are varieties of gifts, but the same Spirit. And there are varieties of ministries, and the same Lord. There are varieties of effects, but the same God who works all things in all persons. But to each one is given the manifestation of the Spirit for the common good. For to one is given the word of wisdom through the Spirit, and to another the word of knowledge according to the same Spirit; to another faith by the same Spirit, and to another gifts of healing by the one Spirit, and to another the effecting of miracles, and to another prophecy, and to another the distinguishing of spirits, to another various kinds of tongues, and to another the interpretation of tongues. But one and the same Spirit works all these things, distributing to each one individually just as He wills.

THE GIFT OF PROPHECY

"No prophecy ever came by human will,
but men and women moved by the Holy Spirit spoke from God."
—2 Peter 1:21 (NRSV)

I. THE GIFT OF PROPHECY DEFINED

A. Kenneth Hagin (late father of the Word of Faith movement)

Prophecy is a supernatural utterance in a *known* tongue.… The Hebrew meaning of the phrase, "to prophecy" is *to flow forth*. It also carries with it the thought: *to bubble forth like a fountain, to let drop, to lift up, to tumble forth,* and *to spring forth.* The Greek word that is translated "prophesy" means *to speak for another.* So "prophesy" can mean to speak for God or to be His spokesman.[1]

B. Dick Iverson (author, founding pastor of City Bible Church [Oregon], formerly called Portland Bible Temple)

The gift of prophecy is speaking under the direct supernatural influence of the Holy Spirit. It is becoming God's mouthpiece, to verbalize His words as the Spirit directs. The word "prophecy" used in I Corinthians 12:10, is the Greek word *propheteia,* and means "speaking forth the mind and counsel of God." It is inseparable in its New Testament usage with the concept of direct inspiration of the Spirit.… Prophecy is the very voice of Christ speaking in the Church.[2]

124

C.   Derek Prince (late author, international Bible teacher)

[The gift of prophecy is] the ability to speak, in a language understood by the believer, words that are inspired and given by the Holy Spirit.... Like all the other gifts, it is made possible only by the supernatural operation of the Holy Spirit.... The first purpose is to edify.... To edify simply means "to build up or strengthen."... The second purpose is to exhort, which means "to stimulate, to encourage, to admonish, and to stir up."... The third purpose is to comfort, which, in contemporary words, means "to cheer up."[3]

D.   David Pytches (Anglican bishop, author)

The gift of prophecy...is the special ability that God gives to members of the Body of Christ to receive and to communicate an immediate message of God to his gathered people, a group among them or any one of his people individually, through a divinely anointed utterance.[4]

E.   Sam Storms (author, Bible teacher, former visiting associate professor of theology at Wheaton College)

Prophecy is not based on a hunch, a supposition, an inference, an educated guess or even on sanctified wisdom. Prophecy is not based on personal insight, intuition or illumination. Prophecy is the human *report* of a divine *revelation*.... In 1 Corinthians 14:1, Paul *commanded* us to desire spiritual gifts, "especially that you may prophesy."[5]

F.   Peter Wagner (missiologist, author, apostolic teacher)

The gift of prophecy is the special ability that God gives to certain members of the Body of Christ to receive and communicate an immediate message of God to His people through a divinely anointed utterance (see Luke 7:26; Acts 15:32; 21:9–11; Rom. 12:6; 1 Cor. 12:10, 28; Eph. 4:11–13).[6]

G.   John Wimber (late author, international Vineyard leader)

Prophecy is declaring the message of God to His church for the purpose of edification. It is not a skill, aptitude, or talent. It is the speaking forth of actual words given by the Spirit in a particular situation and it ceases when the words given by the Spirit cease. A prophetic word may be given in a poetic form or even in a song.[7]

II. NEW TESTAMENT EXAMPLES OF THE GIFT OF PROPHECY

A. Prophecy in the Life of Zacharias

The priest Zacharias prophesied concerning the birth of his son, John the Baptist:

> And they made signs to his father, as to what he wanted him called. And he asked for a tablet and wrote as follows, "His name is John." And they were all astonished. And at once his mouth was opened and his tongue loosed, and he began to speak in praise of God. Fear came on all those living around them; and all these matters were being talked about in all the hill country of Judea. All who heard them kept them in mind, saying, "What then will this child turn out to be?" For the hand of the Lord was certainly with him. And his father Zacharias was filled with the Holy Spirit, and prophesied.
> (Luke 1:62–67; see Zacharias's prophecy in verses 68–79)

B. Prophecy upon Being Filled with the Spirit

The gift of prophecy was part of the modus operandi of the church from its inception, and people often received the gift of prophecy along with the gift of tongues as an evidence of the filling of the Holy Spirit:

> And when Paul had laid his hands upon them [new believers in Ephesus], *the Holy Spirit came on them, and they began speaking with tongues and prophesying.*
> (Acts 19:6)

C. Prophecy Used to Reveal and Release Appointed Ministries

By means of prophecies through a body of elders, Timothy was both called and strengthened for his appointed ministry. (In the first Scripture passage, below, notice that Paul advised him to use the prophetic words as weapons of spiritual warfare.)

> Timothy, my son, I am giving you this command in keeping with the prophecies once made about you, so that by recalling them you may fight the battle well, holding on to faith and a good conscience.   (1 Timothy 1:18–19 NIV)

> Do not neglect the spiritual gift within you, which was bestowed on you through prophetic utterance with the laying on of hands by the presbytery.   (1 Timothy 4:14)

The ministries of Barnabas and Saul were revealed in a similar way:

> While they were ministering to the Lord and fasting, the Holy Spirit said, "Set apart for Me Barnabas and Saul for the work to which I have called them."   (Acts 13:2)

In the above account, no prophet is named; gospel writer Luke simply reported that *"the Holy Spirit said"* it (presumably through one of the members of the gathered body).

D.   Prophecy to Provide Preparation and Direction for Paul

The Holy Spirit spoke directly to Paul to prepare him for the pressures of forthcoming events. Then various prophets in the church interpreted the prophetic words they received to mean that he should not proceed into danger; but Paul, based on what he had heard from the Lord, knew he could and should face the risks with courage. All of them, including Paul himself, were hearing that dangers awaited Paul in Jerusalem, and these predictions were accurate.

> *And now, behold, I am going to Jerusalem, constrained by the Spirit, not knowing what will happen to me there, except that the Holy Spirit testifies to me in every city that imprisonment and afflictions await me.* (Acts 20:22–23 ESV)

> *And having sought out the disciples [in Tyre], we stayed there for seven days. And through the Spirit they were telling Paul not to go on to Jerusalem.… We departed and came to Caesarea, and we entered the house of Philip the evangelist, who was one of the seven, and stayed with him. He had four unmarried daughters, who prophesied. While we were staying for many days, a prophet named Agabus came down from Judea. And coming to us, he took Paul's belt and bound his own feet and hands and said, "Thus says the Holy Spirit, 'This is how the Jews at Jerusalem will bind the man who owns this belt and deliver him into the hands of the Gentiles.'" When we heard this, we and the people there urged him not to go up to Jerusalem. Then Paul answered, "What are you doing, weeping and breaking my heart? For I am ready not only to be imprisoned but even to die in Jerusalem for the name of the Lord Jesus." And since he would not be persuaded, we ceased and said, "Let the will of the Lord be done."* (Acts 21:4, 8–14 ESV)

III. PRESENT PURPOSES OF PROPHECY

God is our good Father, and He wants to encourage us and to advise us. For each new generation, He chooses prophets to deliver fresh words to accomplish His purposes, among which, as Paul wrote, are *"edification and exhortation and consolation"* (1 Corinthians 14:3). The following are several present purposes of prophecy.

A.   For Edification

As we noted earlier, *edification* refers to building up people in the faith and enabling them to be more effective in ministry.

B.   For Exhortation, or Encouragement

Exhortation pertains to admonishment and motivation for people to perform good deeds, and it is the same as encouragement. Some prophets have a primary ministry to be true "sons of encouragement." See Hosea 6:1–3 and all of chapter 4 in Paul's first letter to Timothy.

C. For Consolation, or Comfort

Consolation means giving comfort or solace, or alleviating some kind of distress. Through prophetic words, Jesus Christ speaks to us with great personal concern, tenderness, and care.

> *Blessed be the God and Father of our Lord Jesus Christ, the Father of mercies and God of all comfort, who comforts us in all our tribulation, that we may be able to comfort those who are in any trouble, with the comfort with which we ourselves are comforted by God.* (2 Corinthians 1:3–4 NKJV)

D. To Convict and Convince

The gift of prophecy is also used by the Holy Spirit to convict people of sin and to convince them of God's good intentions toward them. This applies both to believers and unbelievers. We read the following in Paul's instruction about the use of the gift in public assemblies:

> *If an unbeliever or an inquirer comes in while everyone is prophesying, they are convicted of sin and are brought under judgment by all, as the secrets of their hearts are laid bare. So they will fall down and worship God, exclaiming, "God is really among you!"* (1 Corinthians 14:24–25 NIV)

E. For Instruction and Learning

While prophecy has been grouped under "Vocal Gifts," it is also a revelatory gift, and God uses it to instruct and teach us:

> *For you can all prophesy in turn so that everyone may be instructed and encouraged.* (1 Corinthians 14:31 NIV)

F. For the Impartation of Gifts

As mentioned above, prophecy can be used to reveal and to release God-appointed ministries. See 1 Timothy 1:18.

G. To Release the Testimony of Jesus

Through His prophets, Jesus stands in the midst of His people to proclaim His words and to inspire us to do His works. Thus, the goal of all true prophetic ministry is to release the testimony of Christ Jesus. Prophetic messages do not draw attention to the speaker, but rather serve as signposts to direct people's attention to Jesus.

> *For the testimony of Jesus is the spirit of prophecy.* (Revelation 19:10)

IV. HOW PROPHECY IS RECEIVED AND EXPRESSED

A. How Prophecies Are Received

1. Through unpremeditated impressions and thoughts.

    Much prophecy "bubbles up" from impressions and thoughts that are spoken out or written down. (See 1 Corinthians 2:9–16.)

2. Through visions or "trances."

    Prophecy is not always received word for word; it often comes in visual form. Visions are mind-pictures by which God communicates using symbols or audible instructions. When God wanted the disciple named Ananias to go to Saul in Damascus, he spoke to Ananias *in a vision.* (See Acts 9:10–16.) Other examples include Isaiah's awe-inspiring vision:

    > *In the year that King Uzziah died, I saw the Lord sitting on a throne, high and lifted up, and the train of His robe filled the temple.*
    > (Isaiah 6:1 NKJV; see also, for example, Numbers 24:1–6)

    A trance is a visionary state in which a person's natural consciousness and volition are suspended and transcended so that God can communicate something important. For example, when Peter was about to be told to put aside his Jewish training on what constituted "uncleanness" and go to the home of a Gentile centurion, God put him into a trance before He spoke to him in a vision:

    > *Peter went up on the housetop about the sixth hour to pray. But he became hungry and was desiring to eat; but while they were making preparations, he fell into a trance; and he saw the sky opened up, and an object like a great sheet coming down, lowered by four corners to the ground, and there were in it all kinds of four-footed animals and crawling creatures of the earth and birds of the air. A voice came to him, "Get up, Peter, kill and eat!" But Peter said, "By no means, Lord, for I have never eaten anything unholy and unclean." Again a voice came to him a second time, "What God has cleansed, no longer consider unholy." This happened three times, and immediately the object was taken up into the sky.* (Acts 10:9–16)

3. Through dreams and night visions.

    One instance is in Genesis 37:5–9, where Joseph had prophetic dreams about his future as a ruler to whom his brothers would bow down. Other scriptural examples include the following:

    > *In the first year of Belshazzar king of Babylon Daniel saw a dream and visions in his mind as he lay on his bed; then he wrote the dream down and related the following summary of it.* (Daniel 7:1)

> *Hear now My words: If there is a prophet among you, I, the Lord, shall make Myself known to him in a vision. I shall speak with him in a dream.*
>
> (Numbers 12:6)

> *It will come about after this that I will pour out My Spirit on all mankind; and your sons and daughters will prophesy, your old men will dream dreams, your young men will see visions. Even on the male and female servants I will pour out My Spirit in those days.* (Joel 2:28–29)

4. Through angelic visitations.

An angel was sent to John to disclose vital revelation:

> *The Revelation of Jesus Christ, which God gave Him to show to His bond-servants, the things which must soon take place; and He sent and communicated it by His angel to His bond-servant John, who testified to the word of God and to the testimony of Jesus Christ, even to all that he saw.*
>
> (Revelation 1:1–2)

Additionally, an angel brought a word to the centurion Cornelius to urge him to invite Peter to come to his home (see Acts 10:1–7, 22), and an angel went to Paul aboard the storm-buffeted ship to reassure him that he and everyone else on that ship would be preserved, a message Paul communicated to the frightened sailors (see Acts 27:23–26).

B. How Prophecies May Be Expressed or Delivered

1. Simply by speaking out. (See 1 Corinthians 14:4, 6, 19.)

2. Through demonstrative actions. (See 1 Samuel 15:26–28; Ezekiel 4; Acts 21:10–11.)

3. In writing.

The apostle John received the entire book of Revelation while he was *"in the Spirit"* (i.e., in a Holy-Spirit-inspired trance) on the island called Patmos:

> *I was in the Spirit on the Lord's day, and I heard behind me a loud voice like the sound of a trumpet, saying, "Write in a book what you see, and send it to the seven churches."*
>
> (Revelation 1:10–11; see also Daniel 7:1; Jeremiah 36:18)

4. Through song, or accompanied by musical instruments.

Something about music releases prophetic inspiration. Even seasoned prophets such as Elisha relied upon it, and so did David:

> *Elisha said, "…But now bring me a minstrel." And it came about, when the minstrel played, that the hand of the Lord came upon [Elisha].*
>
> (2 Kings 3:14–15)

> *David and the commanders of the army set apart for the service some of the*
> *sons of Asaph and of Heman and of Jeduthun, who were to prophesy with*
> *lyres, harps and cymbals.*   (1 Chronicles 25:1)

In our day, we have pastors and prophetic preachers who are skilled musicians and who receive some of their clearest messages while singing or playing the piano. (See also Colossians 3:16; Ephesians 5:19.)

5. Through any number of other creative art forms, such as drama, dancing, and painting.

V. MATURING IN THE GIFT OF PROPHECY

A. Categories of Prophetic Revelation

1. The spirit of prophecy

    The spirit of prophecy refers to those occasions when the Spirit of God encompasses a group of people, and God manifests His presence in the midst of the assembly in such a way that anybody can prophesy, whether or not they otherwise claim to have a gift of prophecy. We see the spirit of prophecy in Scripture in the story of King Saul:

    > *Then Saul sent messengers to take David, but when they saw the compa-*
    > *ny of the prophets prophesying, with Samuel standing and presiding over*
    > *them, the Spirit of God came upon the messengers of Saul; and they also*
    > *prophesied. When it was told Saul, he sent other messengers, and they also*
    > *prophesied. So Saul sent messengers again the third time, and they also*
    > *prophesied.*   (1 Samuel 19:20–21)

2. The gift of prophecy

    The *gift* of prophecy is the primary topic of this lesson of the study guide. (Refer again to 1 Corinthians 12:10; 14:6, 24, 31.)

3. The ministry of prophecy

    People who exercise the gift of prophecy consistently over time have a ministry or calling of prophecy, developing what you could term a "residential" gift, a ministry that is not circumstantial or occasional.

4. The office of a prophet

    Beyond the ministry of prophecy is the office of a prophet, and people may carry the title "prophet" (or "prophetess"). For glimpses of how they operated in the New Testament church, see Acts 13:1–3; 15:32; 21:10–11; 1 Corinthians 12:28–29; Ephesians 2:18–22; 3:4–6; 4:11–13.

    Those in the office of prophet are equippers; they can tell others how the gift works. Lots of people who prophesy can't be considered equippers because they couldn't tell you how the gift works—they just do it (some of them brilliantly). But people in the office of prophet teach and model a prophetic lifestyle.

When we read in 1 Corinthians 12:28 that *"God has appointed in the church, first apostles, second **prophets**, third teachers, then miracles, then gifts of healings, helps, administrations, various kinds of tongues,"* it is the office of prophet that is being referred to.

B. Judging and Discerning Prophecy

Even when prophecy seems straightforward and simple, it cannot be taken at face value. God's bigness can never be contained in a few words spoken by a human being, and every limited human vessel is prone to errors. Paul wrote, *"For we know in part, and we prophesy in part"* (1 Corinthians 13:9).

When the apostle John was an old man, he wrote, *"Beloved, do not believe every spirit, but test the spirits to see whether they are from God; because many false prophets have gone out into the world"* (1 John 4:1).

Discernment is especially important in relation to directive words. Testing prophetic words provides safeguards against bad decisions, and it also is part of the process of prophetic maturation.

All prophecies, regardless of who gives them or how important they seem, should be confirmed according to these nine scriptural tests:

1. Does the revelation edify, exhort, or console?

2. Is it in agreement with God's written Word?

3. Does it exalt Jesus Christ?

4. Does it bear good fruit? Does the character of the prophet bear good fruit?

5. If it predicts a future event, does it come to pass?

6. Does the prophetic word turn people toward God or away from Him?

7. Does it produce liberty or bondage?

8. Does it produce life, or bring death?

9. Does the Holy Spirit bear witness that it is true?[8]

Questions for Reflection

LESSON TWELVE:
THE GIFT OF PROPHECY

(Answers to these questions can be found in the back of the study guide.)

Fill in the Blank

1.   In your own words, define the gift of prophecy:

   _____

   _____

2.   List three purposes of prophecy (at least seven can be found in the lesson):

   _____

   _____

   _____

3.   Starting with the first chapter of Matthew, the first book of the New Testament, read until you find the first example of a prophetic message. Note chapter and verse:

   _____

133

Multiple Choice—Choose the best answer from the list below:

A—message   C—vision

B—mouthpiece   D—judging

4.   Prophecy is speaking under the influence of the Holy Spirit as His _____.

5.   Prophecies can be received in a number of ways, including by means of a _____ or a dream.

True or False

6.   All prophecy should be judged against the Word of God.   **T / F**

7.   Every believer should desire the gift of prophecy.   **T / F**

8.   Prophecies speak only about future events.   **T / F**

Scripture Memorization

Write out and memorize 1 Corinthians 14:3. The following is from the *New International Version*; choose a different Scripture version if you prefer.

The one who prophesies speaks to people for their strengthening, encouraging and comfort.

Closing Exhortation:

FULFILLING THE GREAT COMMISSION TODAY

"All authority has been given to Me in heaven and on earth.
Go therefore and make disciples of all the nations, baptizing them in the name of the Father
and the Son and the Holy Spirit, teaching them to observe all that I commended you;
and lo, I am with you always, even to the end of the age."
—Matthew 28:18–20

People's last words are very important. They are often sharing the one thing that burns in them the most so that it will leave a lasting impression on others. I know. The last word I received from my late my wife, Michal Ann Goll, came in a card (delivered by an angel on her behalf!) that stated, "Never, never, never, never give up!" I carry that card with those piercing words in its blue envelope in my Bible all around the world. Those words still echo in my being these many years later.

How much more should we take the last recorded words of Jesus from Matthew 28:18–20, given above, and have them burn in our own hearts and be the motivation for our lives today! We should also consider these words recorded in Scripture: *"Jesus Christ is the same yesterday and today and forever"* (Hebrews 13:8). This means that Jesus is still working today as He did when He walked the earth, and it means that He will continue to do the works He has been doing.

"Jesus Christ is the same yesterday and today and forever" does not say anything even close to the following statements, which many people seem to think Jesus is saying to us: "What I did yesterday is good enough. It is written down for you to read. I did miracles, signs, and wonders back then, but sorry, guys, I do not do that stuff anymore. You just get to read about those great times!"

To the contrary, Jesus declared bold statements that would be hard to exaggerate, such as *"Truly, truly, I say to you, he who believes in Me, the works that I do, he will do also; and greater works than these he will do; because I go to the Father."* I did not make that up. It comes from John 14:12 in the New Testament.

It is not a line from a futuristic screenplay about an imaginary great adventure. These are the very words of Jesus. He is waiting for us to believe Him so that we can do those *"greater works"—today!*

I have a dream in my heart. I want to see the entire global body of Christ—those who believe that the words of Jesus are true and for today—to arise empowered by the Holy Spirit to "do the stuff"! Not to be famous (give me a break!), and not to have their names in lights, but to do the works of Jesus so that the fame of His name may be spread far and wide and so the glory of the Lord will cover the earth as the waters cover the sea. (See Habakkuk 2:14.) Is my dream too big? Well, I did not make it up, either, because it is God's dream!

I opened this study guide with a short preface called "Just Do It!" Now I am closing it with a short exhortation, "Fulfilling the Great Commission Today." How will the life and message of Jesus Christ have a chance to make an impact on every nation and people group on the face of the earth? How will the world's people truly be changed and discipled? By reading merely about things God did in the past? Is His name "Jehovah 'Was-y'"? Did God reveal Himself as the great "I Was"? I don't think so. He is the great I Am!

Enter into the adventure of your life by receiving and releasing the gifts of the Holy Spirit today! Be empowered for Jesus Christ's sake to make a permanent impact on the world around you by word and by deed with the great, great, great love of God. You have been commissioned to do the works of Jesus through the full operation of all the gifts of the Spirit—today! Blessings to each of you, my fellow laborers.

Now let me pray for you.

⌣

Father, as we close this study guide, *Impacting the World Through Spiritual Gifts,* inspire each believer with the message of hope that his or her life matters, and help them to stir up their spiritual gifts, for the sake of Your kingdom. Bring divine appointments to these friends who have read this book. Lord, may You be magnified in all we do and say. Let the fragrance of Christ be released through our lives and impact all of our family members. Empower us as never before so that Jesus Christ will receive the rewards for His suffering. We thank You for the days in which we live, and we declare, "Jesus, because of You, and because of Your Father and Your Holy Spirit whom You have given to us, the best is yet to come!"

Amen!

—*James W. Goll*

NOTES

Lesson One: What Are the Spiritual Gifts?

1. John Wimber, "Signs and Wonders, MC510," audio teaching based on a class taught for Fuller Theological Seminary (Anaheim, CA: Vineyard Ministries International, 1985).
2. Wimber, "Signs and Wonders" (quoting Mel Robeck), emphasis mine.
3. Dick Iverson, *The Holy Spirit Today* (Portland, OR: City Christian Publishing, 2006), 75.
4. C. Peter Wagner, *Discover Your Spiritual Gifts* (Ventura, CA: Regal Books, 2005), 19.

Lesson Four: The Gift of Discerning of Spirits

1. Kenneth Hagin, *The Holy Spirit and His Gifts* (Tulsa, OK: Kenneth Hagin Ministries, 1991), 109–111.
2. Iverson, *Holy Spirit Today*, 125.
3. Derek Prince, *The Gifts of the Spirit* (New Kensington, PA: Whitaker House, 2007), 88.
4. Ibid., 85.
5. David Pytches, *Spiritual Gifts in the Local Church* (Minneapolis, MN: Bethany House, 1985), 87.
6. Sam Storms, *The Beginner's Guide to Spiritual Gifts* (Minneapolis, MN: Bethany House, 2012), 131.
7. C. Peter Wagner, *Discover Your Spiritual Gifts*, 146.
8. Wimber, "Signs and Wonders."

Lesson Five: The Gift of a Word of Wisdom

1. Hagin, *Holy Spirit and His Gifts*, 102.
2. Iverson, *Holy Spirit Today*, 106.
3. Prince, *Gifts of the Spirit*, 53 (emphasis in the original), 57.
4. Pytches, *Spiritual Gifts*, 92.
5. Storms, *Beginner's Guide*, 46.
6. Wagner, *Discover Your Spiritual Gifts*, 151–152.
7. Wimber, "Signs and Wonders."

Lesson Six: The Gift of a Word of Knowledge

1. Storms, *Beginner's Guide*, 49, emphasis mine.
2. Hagin, *Holy Spirit and His Gifts*, 85.
3. Iverson, *Holy Spirit Today*, 116.
4. Prince, *Gifts of the Spirit*, 73.
5. Pytches, *Spiritual Gifts*, 99.
6. Storms, *Beginner's Guide*, 49, emphasis mine.
7. Wagner, *Discover Your Spiritual Gifts*, 148.
8. Wimber, "Signs and Wonders."

Lesson Seven: The Gift of Faith

1. Hagin, *Holy Spirit and His Gifts*, 118, emphasis in the original.
2. Iverson, *Holy Spirit Today*, 131, emphasis in the original.
3. Prince, *Gifts of the Spirit*, 109.
4. Ibid., see pages 106–109, 114.
5. Pytches, *Spiritual Gifts*, 109.
6. Storms, *Beginner's Guide*, 60–61.
7. Wagner, *Discover Your Spiritual Gifts*, 147.
8. Wimber, "Signs and Wonders."
9. Pytches, *Spiritual Gifts*, 109.

Lesson Eight: The Gifts of Healings

1. Hagin, *Holy Spirit and His Gifts*, 133–134.
2. Iverson, *Holy Spirit Today*, 139.
3. Prince, *Gifts of the Spirit*, 128–129.
4. Pytches, *Spiritual Gifts*, 117.
5. Storms, *Beginner's Guide*, 61–62, 69.
6. Wagner, *Discover Your Spiritual Gifts*, 147.
7. Wimber, "Signs and Wonders."

Lesson Nine: The Workings of Miracles

1. Hagin, *Holy Spirit and His Gifts*, 127–128, 131.
2. Iverson, *Holy Spirit Today*, 151.
3. Prince, *Gifts of the Spirit*, 128, 139, 151–152.
4. Pytches, *Spiritual Gifts*, 114–115.
5. Storms, *Beginner's Guide*, 85, 88. The Grudem definition comes from Wayne Grudem, *Systematic Theology* (Grand Rapids, MI: Zondervan, 1994), 355.
6. Wagner, *Discover Your Spiritual Gifts*, 149.
7. Wimber, "Signs and Wonders."

Lesson Ten: The Gift of Various Kinds of Tongues

1. Hagin, *Holy Spirit and His Gifts*, 149.
2. Iverson, *Holy Spirit Today*, 175.
3. Prince, *Gifts of the Spirit*, 154, 156.
4. Pytches, *Spiritual Gifts*, 62.
5. Storms, *Beginner's Guide*, 152–153.
6. Wagner, *Discover Your Spiritual Gifts*, 151.
7. Wimber, "Signs and Wonders."

Lesson Eleven: The Gift of Interpretation of Tongues

1. Hagin, *Holy Spirit and His Gifts*, 157, emphasis in the original.
2. Iverson, *Holy Spirit Today*, 178.
3. Prince, *Gifts of the Spirit*, 165, 168.
4. Pytches, *Spiritual Gifts*, 73.
5. Storms, *Beginner's Guide*, 194, 193.
6. Wagner, *Discover Your Spiritual Gifts*, 111.
7. Wimber, "Signs and Wonders."
8. See Prince, *Gifts of the Spirit*, 171–173.

Lesson Twelve: The Gift of Prophecy

1. Hagin, *Holy Spirit and His Gifts*, 139, italics in the original.
2. Iverson, *Holy Spirit Today*, 159.
3. Prince, *Gifts of the Spirit*, 176, 182.
4. Pytches, *Spiritual Gifts*, 79.
5. Storms, *Beginner's Guide*, 116, 111, emphasis in the original.
6. Wagner, *Discover Your Spiritual Gifts*, 114.
7. Wimber, "Signs and Wonders."
8. See, for example, Prince, *Gifts of the Spirit*, 203–222.

ANSWERS TO QUESTIONS FOR REFLECTION

Lesson One: What Are the Spiritual Gifts?

1. For an overview, refer to "**I. INTRODUCTORY STATEMENTS.**"
2. (a) for the common good; (b) to form a body (the body of Christ); (c) to accompany the preaching of the gospel
3. (a) sovereignly given; (b) laying on of hands; (c) casting a mantle
4. B—manifestation
5. D—spiritual gifts
6. T
7. T
8. F

Lesson Two: How the Holy Spirit Moves

1. shadows
2. ask; given
3. walk
4. C—kingdom
5. A—grace
6. F
7. F
8. T

Lesson Three: How to Grow in Exercising Spiritual Gifts

1. God
2. special gift
3. edification
4. B—distribution
5. A—community
6. T
7. T
8. T

Lesson Four: The Gift of Discerning of Spirits

1. Jesus Christ
2. Refer to "**I. THE GIFT OF DISCERNING OF SPIRITS DEFINED.**"
3. (a) discerning the Holy Spirit; (b) discerning angels; (c) discerning human spirits; (d) discerning evil spirits
4. B—expose
5. C—know
6. T
7. T
8. F

Lesson Five: The Gift of a Word of Wisdom

1. wisdom
2. Refer to "**I. A WORD OF WISDOM DEFINED.**"
3. (a) Solomon's wisdom about the two mothers disputing over one child (see 1 Kings 3:16–28); (b) Jesus' wisdom regarding the Pharisees' question about paying taxes (see Matthew 22:15–22); (c) the apostles' wisdom that introduced deacons into the early church (see Acts 6:1–7)
4. A—God
5. D—human intellect
6. F
7. T
8. F

Lesson Six: The Gift of a Word of Knowledge

1. word of knowledge
2. Refer to "**I. THE GIFT OF A WORD OF KNOWLEDGE DEFINED.**"
3. (a) conviction; (b) preparation; (c) revealing knowledge about a situation
4. D—revelation
5. C—counsel
6. F
7. F
8. T

Lesson Seven: The Gift of Faith

1. Refer to "**I. THE GIFT OF FAITH DEFINED.**"
2. faith; mountain; doubt; believes; granted
3. plants; utters it aloud
4. C—confidence
5. A—conjunction
6. F
7. F
8. T

Lesson Eight: The Gifts of Healings

1. Refer to "**I. THE GIFTS OF HEALINGS DEFINED.**"
2. Three of the following five options: the laying on of hands and prayer by believers; prayer with anointing with oil; receiving Communion; speaking the Word; special means (e.g., through anointed garments).
3. (a) Those who came for personal healing. (b) Those who brought someone else for healing. (c) Those who came for someone else but sought only the word of Jesus stating that they would be healed.
4. D—healings
5. A—cleansing

6. T
7. F
8. F

Lesson Nine: The Workings of Miracles

1. Refer to "I. THE GIFT OF WORKINGS OF MIRACLES DEFINED."
2. obedience
3. power; workings of powers
4. D—faith
5. A—preaching
6. F
7. T
8. T

Lesson Ten: The Gift of Various Kinds of Tongues

1. Refer to "I. THE GIFT OF VARIOUS KINDS OF TONGUES DEFINED."
2. Three of the following five options: praise; intercession; rebuking the powers of darkness; exhortation, edification, and comfort; a sign for unbelievers.
3. self-sufficiency; pride
4. C—manifestation
5. D—utterance
6. T
7. F
8. T

Lesson Eleven: The Gift of Interpretation of Tongues

1. Refer to "I. THE GIFT OF INTERPRETATION OF TONGUES DEFINED."
2. communicate; dynamic equivalent
3. interpret
4. B—prophecy
5. D—sensitive
6. F
7. F
8. T

Lesson Twelve: The Gift of Prophecy

1. Refer to "I. THE GIFT OF PROPHECY DEFINED."
2. Three of the following seven options: for edification; for exhortation, or encouragement; for consolation, or comfort; to convict and convince; for instruction and learning; for the impartation of gifts; for releasing the testimony of Jesus.
3. Matthew 1:20–21 (Joseph's dream about the unborn Jesus)
4. B—mouthpiece
5. C—vision
6. T
7. T
8. F

RECOMMENDED RESOURCES

Bickle, Mike. *Growing in the Prophetic: A Practical, Biblical Guide to Dreams, Visions, and Spiritual Gifts.* Lake Mary, FL: Charisma House, 2008.

Chavda, Mahesh. *The Hidden Power of Healing Prayer.* Shippensburg, PA: Destiny Image, 2001.

Fortune, Don, and Katie Fortune. *Discover Your God-Given Gifts.* Grand Rapids, MI: Chosen Books, 2009.

Goll, James W. *The Beginner's Guide to Hearing God.* Bloomington, MN: Chosen Books, 2008.

———. *Deliverance from Darkness: The Essential Guide to Defeating Demonic Strongholds and Oppression.* Grand Rapids, MI: Chosen Books, 2010.

———. *Empowered Prayer: 365-Day Personal Prayer Guide.* Shippensburg, PA: Destiny Image, 2009.

———. *Living a Supernatural Life: The Secret to Experiencing a Life of Miracles* (formerly titled *The Beginner's Guide to Signs, Wonders and the Supernatural Life*). Ventura, CA: Regal Books, 2013.

———. *The Lifestyle of a Prophet: A 21-Day Journey to Embracing Your Calling.* Grand Rapids, MI: Chosen Books, 2013.

———. *The Prophetic Intercessor: Releasing God's Purposes to Change Lives and Influence Nations.* Grand Rapids, MI: Chosen Books, 2007.

———. *Releasing Spiritual Gifts Today.* New Kensington, PA: Whitaker House, 2016.

———. *The Seer: The Prophetic Power of Visions, Dreams, and Open Heavens.* Rev. ed. Shippensburg, PA: Destiny Image, 2012.

Goll, James W. and Michal Ann Goll. *Angelic Encounters.* Lake Mary, FL: Charisma House, 2007.

———. *Dream Language: The Prophetic Power of Dreams, Revelations, and the Spirit of Wisdom.* Shippensburg, PA: Destiny Image, 2006.

Goll, James W., and Michal Ann Goll, Jeff Jansen, Patricia King, Mickey Robinson, Ryan Wyatt. *Adventures in the Prophetic.* Shippensburg, PA: Destiny Image, 2010.

Hagin, Kenneth. *The Holy Spirit and His Gifts.* 2nd ed. Tulsa, OK: Kenneth Hagin Ministries, 1991.

Ireland, David. *Activating the Gifts of the Holy Spirit.* New Kensington, PA: Whitaker House, 1998.

Iverson, Dick. *The Holy Spirit Today.* Portland, OR: City Bible Publishing, 2006.

Johnson, Bill, and Randy Clark. *The Essential Guide to Healing.* Grand Rapids, MI: Chosen Books, 2011.

Prince, Derek. *The Gifts of the Spirit.* New Kensington, PA: Whitaker House, 2007.

Pytches, David. *Spiritual Gifts in the Local Church.* Minneapolis, MN: Bethany House, 1987.

Sandford, John, and Paula Sandford. *The Elijah Task.* Lake Mary, FL: Charisma House, 2006.

Storms, Sam. *The Beginner's Guide to Spiritual Gifts.* 2nd ed. Minneapolis, MN: Bethany House, 2012.

Sumrall, Lester. *Gifts and Ministries of the Holy Spirit.* New Kensington, PA: Whitaker House, 2005.

Wagner, C. Peter. *Discover Your Spiritual Gifts.* Ventura, CA: Regal Books, 2005.

Wimber, John. "Signs & Wonders & Church Growth" (DVD). Stafford, TX: Vineyard Resources (recorded in the 1980s). (See http://www.vineyardresources.com/equip/.)

OTHER BOOKS BY JAMES W. GOLL

The Call of the Elijah Revolution (by James Goll and Lou Engle)

The Coming Israel Awakening: Gazing into the Future of the Jewish People and the Church

Empowered Women (by James Goll and Michal Ann Goll)

Exploring Your Dreams and Visions: Receive and Understand your Visions, Dreams, and Supernatural Experiences

God Encounters: The Prophetic Power of the Supernatural to Change Your Life

Intercession: The Power and Passion to Shape History

Living a Supernatural Life: The Secret to Experiencing a Life of Miracles

The Lost Art of Intercession: Restoring the Power and Passion of the Watch of the Lord

The Lost Art of Practicing His Presence

The Lost Art of Pure Worship (by James Goll, et al.)

Passionate Pursuit: Getting to Know God and His Word

Prayer Storm: The Hour That Changes the World

A Radical Faith: Essentials for Spirit-Filled Believers

Shifting Shadows of Supernatural Experiences: A Manual to Experiencing God-Empowered Prayer (by James Goll and Julia Loren)

And many more…

In addition, there are numerous study guides available to accompany the books, including *Discovering the Seer in You, Exploring the Nature and Gift of Dreams, Prayer Storm, A Radical Faith, Prophetic Foundations, Walking in the Supernatural Life,* and many others, with corresponding CD and MP3 albums and DVD messages.

For more information:

James W. Goll

Encounters Network

P.O. Box 1653

Franklin, TN 37065

www.encountersnetwork.com ◆ www.prayerstorm.com
www.compassionacts.com ◆ www.GETeSchool.com
info@encountersnetwork.com ◆ inviteJames@gmail.com